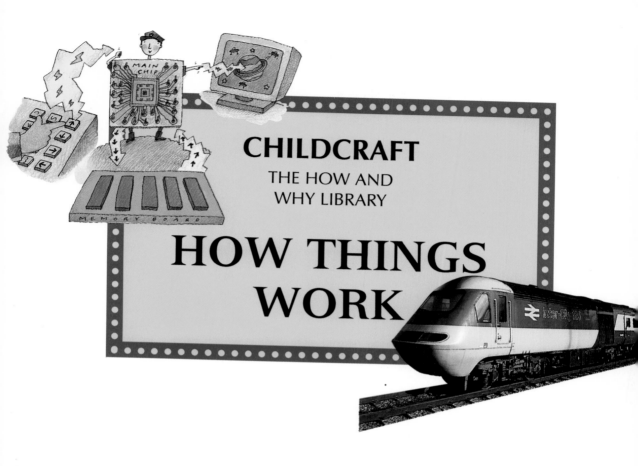

CHILDCRAFT
THE HOW AND WHY LIBRARY

HOW THINGS WORK

World Book, Inc.
a Scott Fetzer company
Chicago

Childcraft—The How and Why Library
(Reg. U.S. Pat. and T.M. Off.—Marca Registrada)
© 2000 World Book, Inc. All rights reserved. This volume may not
be reproduced in whole or in part in any form without prior written
permission from the publisher.

World Book, Inc.
233 N. Michigan Avenue
Chicago, IL 60601

© 1996, 1995, 1994, 1993, 1991, 1990, 1989, 1987, 1986, 1985
World Book, Inc. © 1982, 1981, 1980, 1979, World Book-Childcraft
International, Inc. © 1976, 1974, 1973, 1971, 1970, 1969, 1968, 1965,
1964 Field Enterprises Educational Corporation.

International Copyright © 1996, 1995, 1994, 1993, 1991, 1990, 1989,
1987, 1986, 1985 World Book, Inc. International Copyright © 1982,
1981, 1980, 1979 World Book-Childcraft International, Inc. International
Copyright © 1976, 1974, 1973, 1971, 1970, 1969, 1968, 1965, 1964
Field Enterprises Educational Corporation.

Childcraft—The How and Why Library ISBN 0-7166-0197-4
How Things Work ISBN 0-7166-0158-3
Library of Congress Catalog Card Number 98-75114
Printed in the United States of America
1 2 3 4 5 6 7 8 9 06 05 04 03 02 01 00

**For information on other World Book products,
visit our Web site at www.worldbook.com
For information on sales to schools and libraries in the
United States, call 1-800-975-3250.
For information on sales to schools and libraries in
Canada, call 1-800-837-5365.**

Contents

Introduction **4**

Inventions in the Home **8**
People didn't always have handy things like zippers
and toothbrushes. What other kinds of helpful
inventions surround us?

On the Move **44**
Many different kinds of vehicles and machines help people and
things move around the earth. Find out how some of them work.

Signals in the Air **84**
When you listen to a CD or watch TV, the sounds you hear and
the pictures you see have traveled through the air, like waves on
the ocean. How do they do that?

Raw Materials **110**
Raw materials are the ingredients used to make
something. Find out what paper, action figures,
and many other things are made of.

Creating and Designing **150**
Look around you. Are there buildings, bridges,
cars, or roads? Who designed them and how did
they do it?

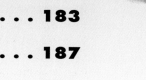

Answers **180**

Glossary **183**

Index **187**

Illustration Acknowledgments . . **191**

Introduction

You probably don't think about it often, but your world is filled with tools and machines that make your life easier. Imagine an average school day and think of all the gadgets and inventions you use.

Your alarm clock rings. You get out of bed. You turn on the light, use the toilet, and take a shower. You blow-dry your hair, then pull on your clothes. You grab the milk from the refrigerator and fix a piece of toast. You catch the bus for school. At school, your teacher shows a videotape, and you do some math problems on the computer. After school, your mom drives you to the mall. Some friends are there, and you ride up and down the escalator and check out the newest CD's in the music store. Your parents cook dinner in the microwave. After dinner, you call your friend to discuss tomorrow's spelling test.

Now imagine that you are living about 150 years ago instead of today. Your alarm clock is a rooster. Your house probably does not have indoor plumbing, so you pump water from a well and go to the outhouse when you need to use the bathroom. You have no electricity for light bulbs, a hairdryer, a refrigerator, a toaster, a VCR, a computer, an escalator, a CD player, a microwave, or a telephone, and those things do not exist. To go anywhere, you walk or ride in a horse-drawn carriage because there are no cars or buses.

This book, *How Things Work,* takes a closer look at all kinds of modern gadgets and inventions that make life easier. You'll learn about machines you use at home and vehicles for getting around. You'll examine materials used to make wonderful things. You'll learn about creating and designing homes, tunnels, and bridges. And you'll find out about jobs that people do to help make things.

There are many features in this book to help you find your way through it. You will find fun-filled facts in the boxes marked **Know It All!** You can amaze your friends with what you learn!

This book also has many activities that you can do at home. Look for the words **Try This!** over a colored ball. The activity that follows offers a way to learn more

Know It All! boxes have fun-filled facts.

Each activity has a number. The higher the number, the more adult help you may need.

An activity that has this colorful border is a little more complex than one without the border.

about how things work. For example, you can discover a tricky way to make a piece of clay float in water, build a fan with a spinning turbine blade, or turn pulp into paper.

Each activity has a number in its colored ball. Activities with a 1 in a green ball are simplest to do. Those with a 2 in a yellow ball may require adult help with tasks such as cutting, measuring, or using hot water. Activities with a 3 in a red ball may need more adult help.

A Try This! activity that has a colorful border around its entire page is a little more complex or requires a few more materials. Take a moment to review the list of materials needed and to read the instructions before you begin.

As you read this book, you will see that some words are printed in bold type, **like this.** These are words that might be new to you. You can find the meanings and pronunciations of these words in the **Glossary**. Turn to the **Index** to look up page numbers of subjects that interest you the most.

If you enjoy learning how things work, find out more in other resources. Here are just a few. Check them out at a bookstore or at your local or school library.

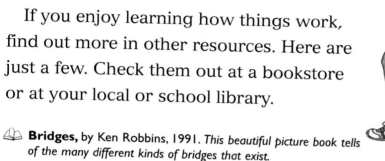

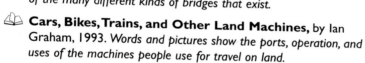

Bridges, by Ken Robbins, 1991. *This beautiful picture book tells of the many different kinds of bridges that exist.*

Cars, Bikes, Trains, and Other Land Machines, by Ian Graham, 1993. *Words and pictures show the ports, operation, and uses of the machines people use for travel on land.*

Cheese, by Linda Illsley, 1990. *This book will tell you all about cheese and how it is made.*

Floating in Space, by Franklyn Branley, 1998. *Read this book and find out how astronauts float in space.*

How Stuff Works, http://www.bygpub.com/HowStuffWorks *This Web site explains how things work in the world around you.*

The Internet for Kids, by Charnan and Tom Kazunas, 1997. *In this book, you will learn about the Internet and how it works.*

Kermit Learns Windows, by Kathleen Resnick, 1993. *Spend some time with Kermit and learn how to use a computer.*

Magic School Bus Fun Place, http://www.scholastic.com/ MagicSchoolBus *Ms. Frizzle, that popular zany science teacher, takes you on educational field trips in her traveling bus.*

Make it Work! science series, by World Book, Inc. *This innovative series offers young scientists facts and experiments on such topics as buildings, flight, machines, photography, ships, sound, and time.*

The New Way Things Work, by David Macaulay, 1998. *With detailed illustrations, this volume shows you how hundreds of machines work, including those using digital technology.*

Rice, by Pam Robson, 1997. *In this book you will learn how rice is grown, processed, and eaten around the world.*

Inventions in the Home

Every day we use things that make our lives easier. We flip a switch to turn on the lights. We turn on the faucet and fill a glass with water. Our clothes have zippers and snaps that make getting dressed easier. We have alarm clocks to wake us.

What would life be like without lamps or zippers? How would you clean your teeth without a toothbrush or dental floss? Our homes are filled with all sorts of helpful inventions. Can you name some of the things that make our lives easier?

electric
light bulb

telescope

television

portable radio

Which Inventions Don't Belong?

TRY THIS!

Some **inventions** we have today have been around for a long time. Others are improved versions of older inventions that are even easier to use. This picture is a house from the early 1900's. Your great-great

electric fan

telephone

piano

chair

frozen food

digital camera

grandparents may have lived in a house without electricity. That means they also would not have had electric light bulbs. What other things in the above picture do you think weren't around in the early 1900's?

See page 180 for answers.

Great Idea!

Some inventions are simple, like these adhesive bandages.

Inventors (ihn VEHN tuhrz) are people who make things that make our lives easier.

Many inventions are simple. In 1865, S. E. Pettee invented a machine for making paper bags. Earle Dickson invented the first ready-to-use bandage in 1920. Some inventions take many years to develop. The great artist Leonardo da Vinci made drawings of his ideas about 500 years ago. He drew an airplane, a parachute, and a helicopter. It was more than 300 years before any of these were made.

Thomas A. Edison invented the first light bulb in 1879. But several other men worked on similar designs before Edison did.

Leonardo da Vinci was an inventor. He drew this design for a parachute, *right*, 300 years before one was made.

To keep their ideas safe and prove they thought of it first, inventors apply for a patent. The patent gives the inventor the right to make his invention or sell his idea. Edison had more patents than anyone else—he had 1,093!

KNOW It All!

Hot or Cold?

Are you hot or cold? A **thermometer** (thuhr MOM uh tuhr) will take your temperature. There are many different kinds. Take your pick.

One type of thermometer has a thin glass tube partially filled with liquid. When the air is warm, the liquid in the tube becomes warm and rises. It rises because heat makes a liquid expand, or take up more space. The warmer it gets, the more space it needs. When the temperature drops, the liquid contracts, or takes up less space, so it moves down the tube. The liquid in many thermometers is a silver-colored metal called mercury. Some thermometers are filled with colored alcohol.

A digital thermometer has a metal probe. When the thermometer is turned

on, a battery inside sends around an electric current. If the probe is warm, the current will move easily. If the probe is cool, the current will not move as easily. The thermometer shows a temperature reading based on how easily the current moves.

Doctors often use an IR thermometer to detect **infrared** (ihn fruh REHD) rays from a person's eardrum. The hotter you are, the more radiation the thermometer detects. The thermometer converts the amount of radiation to a temperature reading.

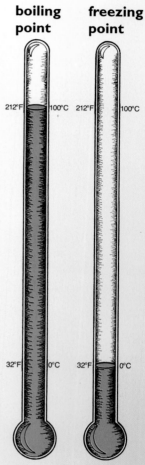

boiling point **freezing point**

212°F 100°C 212°F 100°C

32°F 0°C 32°F 0°C

A standard thermometer contains a liquid that moves up when it becomes warm. The liquid drops down when it cools. The lines indicate the temperature.

Chillin'

Just a few minutes after you put warm food in a refrigerator, the food feels cooler. The refrigerator carries the heat from the food into the room outside.

How does a refrigerator do this? When a liquid changes to a gas it **evaporates** (ih VAP uh rayts). As it evaporates, it takes heat from the things around it. Also, when a gas changes to a liquid, it **condenses**

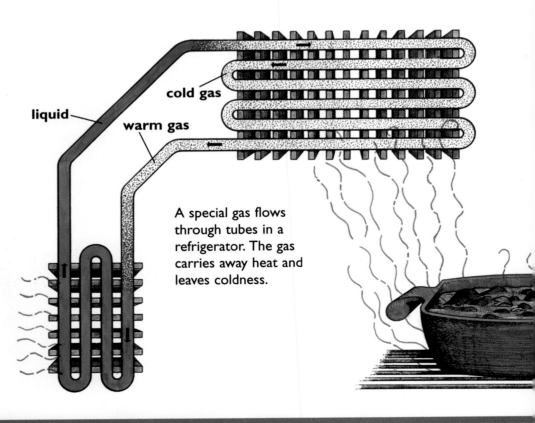

cold gas

liquid

warm gas

A special gas flows through tubes in a refrigerator. The gas carries away heat and leaves coldness.

(kuhn DEHN suhz), and gives off heat.

Refrigerators are cooled by a special liquid that is easily turned into a gas and then back to a liquid. First, the cool liquid is pumped to tubes inside the refrigerator, where it evaporates. As the liquid changes to a gas, it takes heat from the air inside the refrigerator. This makes the refrigerator cooler.

Then the warm gas is pumped into tubes outside the refrigerator, where it condenses. As the gas changes back to a liquid, it gives off heat. When the liquid cools, it is pumped back into the refrigerator. There it evaporates again. In and out it goes, carrying heat from the refrigerator and keeping the food cold.

KNOW It All!

Do you ever feel chilled when you get out of the bathtub or after swimming? This is because the water on your skin is evaporating off your body. It goes into the air where you can't see it. As this happens, it takes heat away from your body, making you feel chilled.

Water vapor in the air sometimes clings to objects. On a hot day water vapor sticks to a cold glass of water. As more vapor sticks to the glass, it condenses, forming droplets of water on the outside of the glass.

Popping Up!

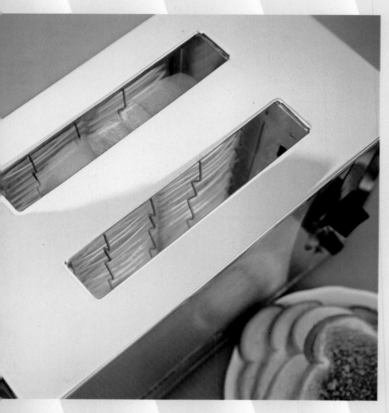

As the metal switch inside a toaster heats, it expands, pushing the hook holding the rack. Up pops your toast!

Toast is tasty for breakfast or a snack. And with a toaster, it's so easy to make.

First, you put a slice of bread in each toaster slot. A rack holds it in place. Then you push down the lever. The lever is connected to the rack and to a spring. The spring unwinds, but a hook holds the rack down. The heat turns on. The coils inside each slot glow orange.

The heat from the coils toasts the bread. It also heats a metal switch. The switch is made from two types of metal. One type expands from the heat. The other does not. As one half of the metal expands, the switch bends. When it bends, it moves a small bar. This bar pushes against the hook. The rack is released. The spring makes the rack and the toast pop up!

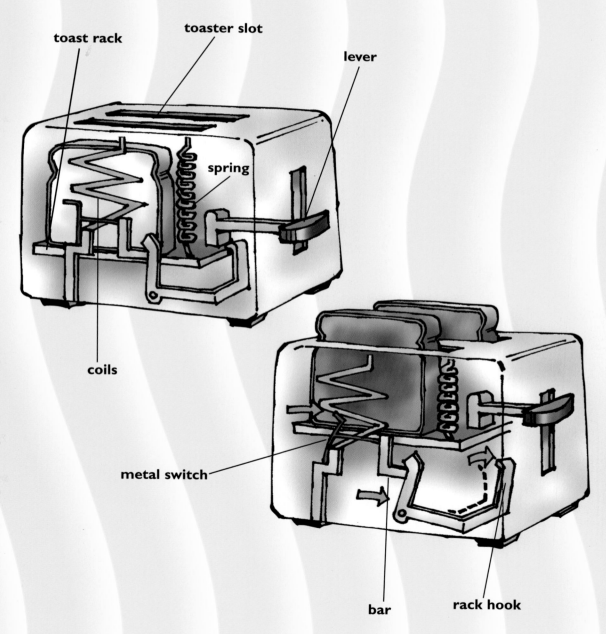

toast rack

toaster slot

lever

spring

coils

metal switch

bar

rack hook

Front-loading machines, *opposite page*, tumble the clothes through soapy water. A top-loading machine, *below*, has an agitator (AJ uh tay tuhr) in the center. Fins on the agitator move the clothes around in the water to clean them.

Clothes on the Move!

Are your favorite jeans dirty? No problem. Put them in the washer. They'll be clean and ready to wear in no time. When people washed clothes by hand, it took all day. After the clothes were washed, each item had to be twisted to wring out the water.

Today, a washing machine does all the work. First you choose the wash setting. Then you add your clothes and detergent. When you turn the machine on, the machine fills the washing basket, or drum, with water. A

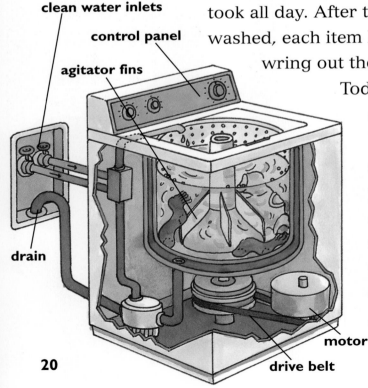

clean water inlets

control panel

agitator fins

drain

motor

drive belt

tiny computer chip, called a **sensor** (SEHN suhr) shuts off the waterflow when the level is high enough.

The clothes twist or tumble about in the soapy water. When the clothes are clean, a pump drains the dirty water from the machine. Then the rinse cycle fills the drum with clean water. When the rinse water is pumped out, the timer switches the motor to a faster speed, and the drum spins very quickly. The clothes are flung against the sides of the drum. The water is forced out of the clothes and pumped down the drain. Now your clothes are ready for the dryer.

water level sensor

water flows in

pump

water flows out

motor

TRY THIS!
1

Which is the better washer? You or your washing machine? Try this clothes-cleaning challenge to find out. Find two old socks or two rags made from the same fabric. Make a stain on each sock or rag using about a teaspoon of grape juice or mustard. Wash one sock with a load of clothes in the washing machine. Wash the other sock by hand, using the same detergent. Is one sock cleaner than the other? Which way is most efficient?

A Dirty Job

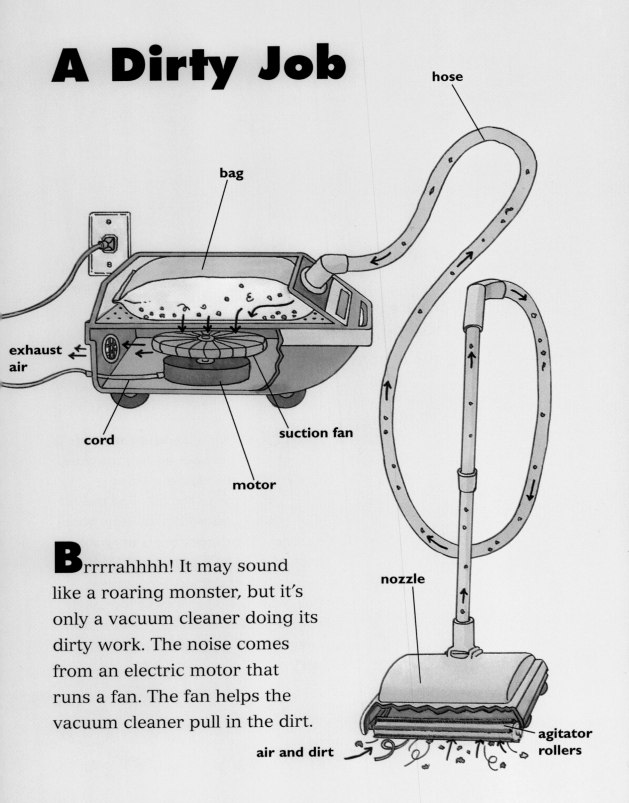

hose

bag

exhaust
air

cord

suction fan

motor

nozzle

air and dirt

agitator
rollers

Brrrrahhhh! It may sound
like a roaring monster, but it's
only a vacuum cleaner doing its
dirty work. The noise comes
from an electric motor that
runs a fan. The fan helps the
vacuum cleaner pull in the dirt.

When you drink through a straw, you create a vacuum. This activity will show you how empty space creates a vacuum. Place a plastic drinking straw in a glass of water. Cover the opening on top of the straw with your finger. Keeping the straw covered, lift it from the glass. What happens?

When you cover the air opening, a vacuum is made. So, when you lift the straw from the glass, the vacuum also holds the water in the straw. Now drop a few rice grains into the glass. Can you use the straw to pick up or "vacuum up" each grain of rice? Do not use your mouth.

When you turn on the vacuum cleaner, the fan starts. It draws air from the bottom of the vacuum cleaner up into the dust bin or bag. As the air moves up, it leaves an empty space at the bottom of the vacuum cleaner. Any empty space is called a vacuum. That's how the vacuum cleaner got its name.

A brush at the bottom of the cleaner helps loosen dirt in the rug. This brush is called a beater brush. A rubber belt connects the brush to the motor. As the motor spins, the brush spins and makes the rug vibrate. The vibration loosens the dirt. The vacuum pulls more air and dirt into the dust bin or bag.

When the dust bin gets full, it is emptied. Or, when the bag gets full, it is thrown away and replaced with a fresh bag.

Hot Air

With a hairdryer, we don't have to wait for our hair to dry.

Electricity travels on a pathway of wire. The electricity travels easily on most of the wire in the pathway. This is called **conducting** (kuhn DUHK tihng) electricity. The path is open. The electrons in the wire are free to move.

But some metals **resist** (rih ZIHST), or slow down, the electric current. When the electrons slow down, they bump into one another as they move through the wire.

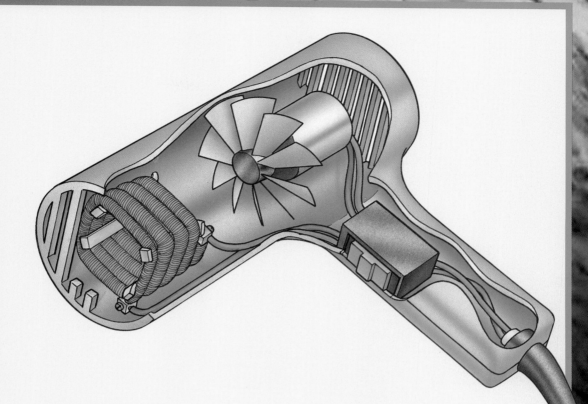

Then the wire heats up. The harder they bump and push, the hotter the wire gets.

When you plug in a hairdryer and turn it on, electricity travels through it. It powers a tiny fan. Then the electricity travels to coiled wire made of resistant metals. These wires heat up. The fan blows heat from these wires out through a vent. This is the hot air that dries your hair.

Inside an electric hairdryer, you can see the coiled wire that heats up. The fan blows the heat out to dry your hair.

Down the Drain

You probably don't think of a toilet as a machine. But that's what it is. You press down the flush lever, and the toilet does the work.

Most toilets have two main parts—a tank and a bowl. The tank sits on the back of the toilet bowl. Both contain water. The bottom of the tank has an opening with a

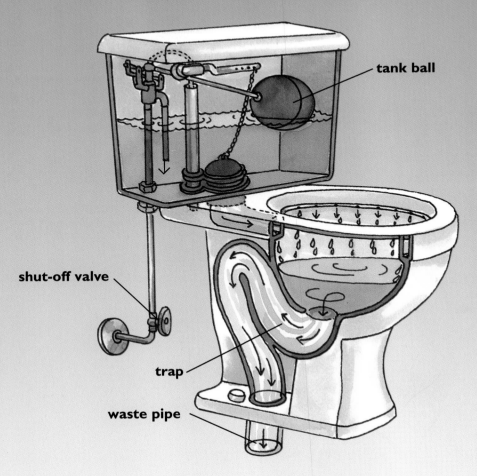

tank ball

shut-off valve

trap

waste pipe

TRY THIS!

2

It's hard to see how the water in a toilet leaves the tank and enters the bowl. This activity will allow you to watch your toilet in action. Ask an adult for permission first. Then ask for help to remove the lid from the toilet tank. Drop a few tablespoons of poppy seeds in the tank. Replace the tank lid. Now flush the toilet. Watch the poppy seeds ride the flow of water from the tank and down the drain. It may take several flushes before all the poppy seeds are gone.

plug. The plug keeps the water in the tank from flowing into the bowl. Pushing down the lever to flush the toilet lifts up the plug.

Water then rushes out of the tank. It flows into the toilet bowl through small holes all around the rim of the bowl.

The fresh water pushes the dirty water into the drain pipe. The plug closes when the tank is empty. Fresh water then flows through an inlet tube into the tank. And the tank is ready for the next flush.

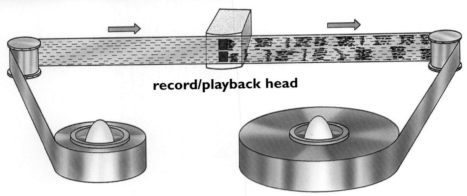

record/playback head

magnetic tape

To record or to play back sound, a magnetic tape passes over the record or playback head. Tiny magnetic patterns tell the machine what sounds to play back or record.

Play It Again!

How are sounds saved on tape? The recording tape acts like a magnet. The tape is a ribbon of plastic coated with iron oxide powder, a material that can be magnetized easily.

When you record something, sound is changed into electrical signals. These signals are sent to the pickup, or recording, head. The recording head arranges the iron oxide powder on the tape into tiny magnetic patterns.

When you want to play back your recording, the tape goes past a replay head. The replay head reads the pattern and turns it into electrical signals. The signals go to an **amplifier** (AM pluh FY uhr). That makes the electrical signals stronger. Then they pass to speakers or headphones. Here they are turned back into sound.

Cassettes can be played again and again. When new sounds are recorded on a tape, the magnet pattern is changed to match the new sounds. The tape passes along an erase head that removes the old pattern. Then it goes to the recording head, where the iron oxide is arranged into a new pattern.

A videotape works like a cassette tape, but it is much wider. A cassette tape records only sound, but a videotape records pictures as well as sound.

videotape

TRY THIS!

1

Ask your parents for old cassette and videotapes that you can take apart. Remove the plastic case. What do you find inside? How is the cassette tape different from the videotape? How are they similar?

audiotape

A videotape works like a cassette tape. It has two reels of tape inside a case.

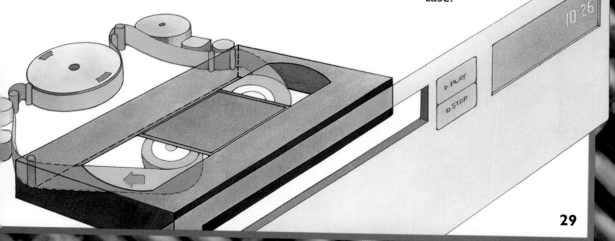

Giving Sound a Spin

Cassette tapes sound good when they are new. But after a while, they sound scratchy. A compact disc, or CD, produces much better sound. It is played using a special light called a **laser beam** (LAY zuhr beem). Only the beam of light touches the CD, so it stays like new.

Sound on a CD is stored in a digital code, like the type of code that computers use. When a CD is made, a microphone turns sound **vibrations** (vy BRAY shunz) into electrical signals, then a machine changes the signals into a digital code.

A powerful laser cuts tiny pits into the surface of a blank compact disc.

This code is fed into a powerful laser. As a blank disc turns, the laser cuts billions of tiny pits into the surface of the disc.

Inside a CD player is another laser. It is not powerful enough to cut the surface of the disc. When the CD is played, the laser reads the position of the pits—a digital code. As the CD turns, it reads from the center to the edge of the disc. These pulses of light are turned into electrical signals. The signals make the speakers **vibrate** (VY brayt). Then you hear the sounds.

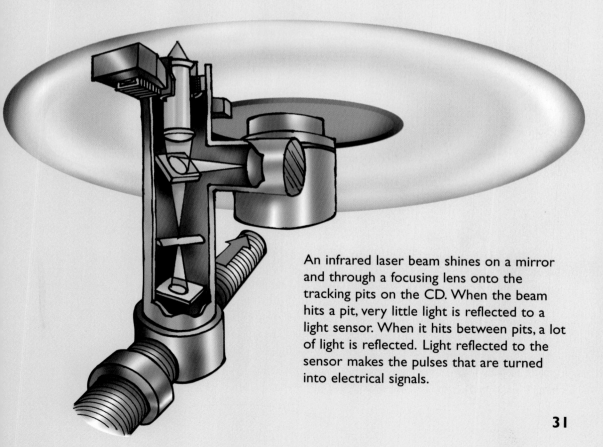

An infrared laser beam shines on a mirror and through a focusing lens onto the tracking pits on the CD. When the beam hits a pit, very little light is reflected to a light sensor. When it hits between pits, a lot of light is reflected. Light reflected to the sensor makes the pulses that are turned into electrical signals.

Is It Real?

Look at a picture of yourself. Now look at it from a different angle. Do you see another side of yourself in the picture? No,

Does this shark look real? It's a hologram—projected underwater to look like the real thing.

but if you were looking at a hologram you could walk around the picture and see the left side of your body, your back, your right side, your front, and the top of your head.

A hologram is an image that looks three-dimensional—that is, it seems to have depth, height, and width. Some credit cards have holograms on them. Holograms also appear in advertisements, artwork, and jewelry.

A hologram is made with laser beams. A laser beam is a kind of colored light. One laser beam is bounced off a mirror then off the subject and onto a special film. Another laser beam is also bounced off a mirror and onto the film. Where the two beams cross on the film, they make a tiny pattern of bright and dark stripes, a hologram.

Guiding a laser beam onto the film will produce light rays that seem to come from the original subject. The resulting three-dimensional image appears to hover in space. You can look over, under, and around the subject. When a hologram is viewed with regular light or sunlight, the image appears with rainbowlike bands of color.

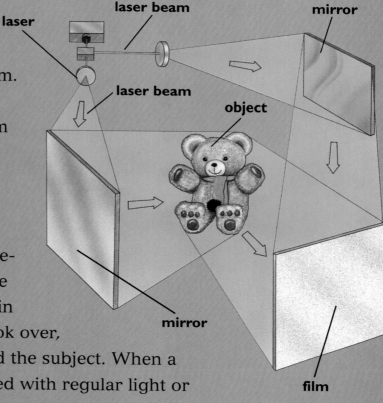

laser **laser beam** **mirror**

laser beam

object

mirror

film

To make a hologram of an object, such as this teddy bear, a laser is aimed into a mirror then at the object. Another laser is reflected off a mirror and then onto the film. The film records the hologram.

TRY THIS!

Hold a pencil or other small object in front of you. Cover or close one eye and look at the object. Then cover the other eye and look at it. What happens to the object? Does it seem to move? Our eyes are a couple of inches apart. So each eye gets a slightly different view. The two views blend into one picture. What we see with both eyes has depth, height, and width—all three dimensions.

Power Processing

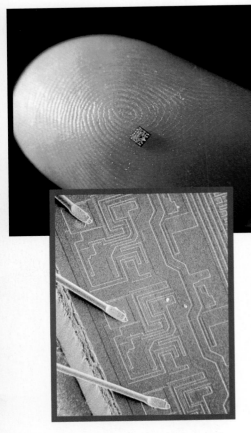

The most important part of a computer is its microchip, or integrated circuit. A microchip can fit on a fingertip. When seen under a microscope, the tiny grooves and wires look like a maze.

Telephones have them. Most watches have them. They help make our cars safe. They make our telephones work more quickly. And space travel would be impossible without them.

They are **microprocessors** (MY kroh PRAH sehs uhrz). They make our lives easier in many ways. A microprocessor fits into a **microchip** and can hold all the signals needed to run electronic devices. A microchip can store information, or figure things out, then it's called a microprocessor. A microprocessor works faster than your brain. And it can fit on the tip of your finger!

The surface of this tiny part is cut with grooves. Each groove is packed with thousands of tiny electrical switches. The switches are connected by thin metal wires. All the wires link

All of these things use microprocessors.

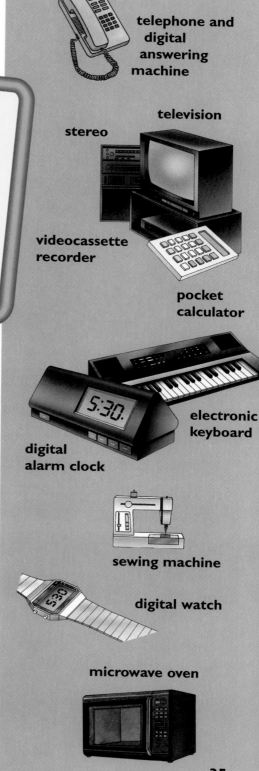

telephone and digital answering machine

television

stereo

videocassette recorder

pocket calculator

electronic keyboard

digital alarm clock

5:30.

sewing machine

digital watch

microwave oven

The first integrated circuit was made for the U.S. space program in 1959. Equipment on the spacecraft had to be very small. All electrical signals for the equipment were put on a strip of material called **silicon** (SIHL uh kuhn). Later, circuits were made into tiny squares called silicon chips.

together—a group called a **circuit** (SIHR kiht).

Microprocessors are also called **integrated circuits** (IHN tuh GRAY tihd SIHR kihts). Equipment like **calculators** (KAHL kyuh LAY tuhrz) made with integrated circuits are small, light, and easy to use.

When you use such equipment, bursts of electric currents speed along the circuits. These bursts are like messages. They tell the equipment what to do.

Zeroing in

As electricity moves through the circuits in the computer, millions of tiny switches are turned on and off. The computer reads a code of zeros and ones. Think of the code as switches in a line. The ones are switches that are turned on, the zeros are switches that are turned off.

The code is called digital. Because it uses only two numbers in different patterns, it is also called binary code. When you type an A on the keyboard, the computer stores the A in its memory as 01000001. Each time you click the mouse, or press a key, it is changed to binary code and stored in the computer's memory.

Do you know what this message says? Use the code to translate it. It is three words.

01001111   01001110

01000001   01001110   01000100

01001111   01000110   01000110

Each letter of the alphabet has a code number made from ones and zeros.

A	01000001
B	01000010
C	01000011
D	01000100
E	01000101
F	01000110
G	01000111
H	01001000
I	01001001
J	01001010
K	01001011
L	01001100
M	01001101
N	01001110
O	01001111
P	01010000
Q	01010001
R	01010010
S	01010011
T	01010100
U	01010101
V	01010110
W	01010111
X	01011000
Y	01011001
Z	01011010

See page 180 for answer.

Computer Bits

Computers save us a lot of work—and a lot of time. The processor of the computer follows step-by-step instructions—exactly and quickly. This series of steps is called a program. A program might be thousands of steps long, but the processor can run the program in less than a second.

The program is stored in the computer's memory. It is stored as a series of 1's and 0's. This is called a **digital code** (DIHJ uh tuhl kohd).

Sometimes the code is stored on a CD-ROM or inside the

This girl uses a computer in a school classroom. Students practice geography, history, math, typing, and reading while learning computer skills.

Laser printers are the fastest printers. A beam of laser light makes an electrically charged image on a rotating cylinder. The charged areas attract powdered or liquid ink, called toner, onto the cylinder. The cylinder transfers the toner with the image onto the paper. The paper then passes through fuser rollers. These rollers seal the toner to the page so it doesn't smear.

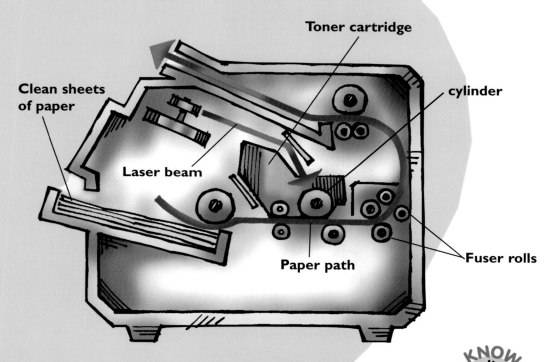

Toner cartridge

Clean sheets of paper

cylinder

Laser beam

Paper path

Fuser rolls

computer on the hard drive. But the computer finds it when it needs it.

When you have finished a report, you tell the computer to print it. The computer sends the digital code to the printer. The printer has a microprocessor that changes the code into letters—so you and your teacher can read it.

Disc Delivery

CD-ROM's are important tools for computer users. CD-ROM's are discs that store words, music, and images. Encyclopedias, games, and other programs that would require up to a dozen floppy disks can fit onto one CD-ROM. CD-ROM stands for compact disc read-only memory.

When you put a CD-ROM into your computer's drive, files are copied from the disc to the computer's hard drive. These files tell the computer how to access all the information on the CD-ROM.

A DVD (digital video disc) is the same size as a CD-ROM but can store much more information. Unlike a CD or CD-ROM, the DVD is able to record data (information) on both the top and the bottom of the plastic disc. And it can record two layers of data on each side. A DVD player can also play CD-ROM's.

Information is burned onto a DVD using a laser, just like CD's and CD-ROM's are made. The bumps and pits on a DVD, left, are much smaller than those made on CD's, right, and CD-ROM's. The information is also on two levels. Two lasers are needed to "read" the information—one for each level.

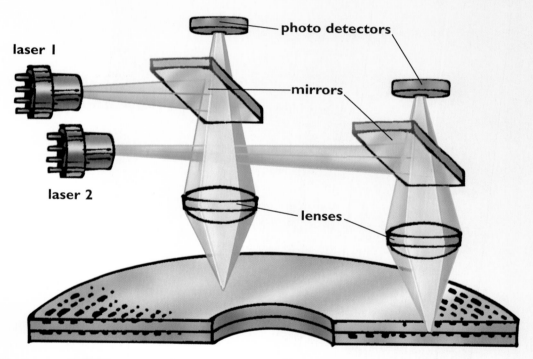

A DVD contains layers of digital data encoded in tiny pits. In a DVD player, a lens focuses a laser beam on the desired layer. As the disc rotates, the pits and the flat areas between them reflect patterns of light to a photo detector, which changes the patterns into electrical signals. A single layer of a DVD has more pits, placed closer together, than an ordinary CD has, and so can store more data.

wagon

fan

paint roller

tandem bike

sprinkler

sewing machine

lawn mower

computer

grill

TRY THIS!

1

What Machines Do They Need?

Imagine life without all the machines and inventions we use every day. Life would be much easier for the people shown if they had the right machines. For example, the boy carrying an hourglass could be wearing a watch instead. Can you figure out what they need to make their lives easier?

See page 180 for answers.

watch

On the Move

Machines are great at home. But they also help us move things—and people—from one place to another. With the help of machines, people can go almost anywhere! They can move people or things around a building, across a continent, or over the ocean.

These machines use wheels, propellers, engines, and more. Keep reading to find out how these machines work!

Machines that Move Things

Some machines move people. Some machines move things. All the machines shown here move people or things. They make peoples' lives easier. Read each clue. Can you tell which machine it describes?

See page 180-181 for answers.

mixer

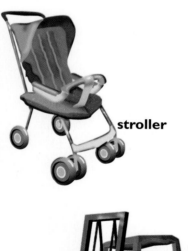

stroller

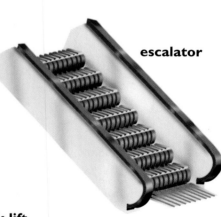

escalator

fork lift

tractor-semitrailer

1. When its wheel spins, it helps turn clay into something else.
2. This rolling machine makes it easy to carry and move things at a grocery store.
3. This has no hands, but it uses a magnet to lift and set down heavy things.
4. This machine is like a moving staircase.
5. This machine helps grown-ups move a baby through a park, a store, or almost anywhere.
6. This machine doesn't just move things; it beats them.
7. This machine can carry many kinds of things fast and far.
8. Step into this machine and press a button. When you get where you're going, the doors will open.
9. This belt carries things through a factory, but it won't hold up your jeans.
10. You use a simple kind of this machine to put food in your mouth.

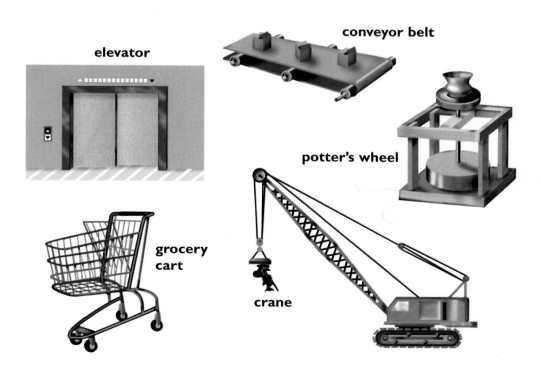

elevator

conveyor belt

potter's wheel

grocery cart

crane

Movin' on up!

Shopping in a big department store is fun. But lugging bags up and down stairs is not! **Escalators** (EHS kuh LAY turhrz) are stairs that move. They make it easy to get to different levels. When you stand on an escalator step, it carries you up one level, or down one level. The steps on an escalator

stair in folded position

stair in raised position

gear turning belt

48

gear turning belt

motor turning gears

move around and around on a huge belt that carries them up and down. A motor turns the belt.

Step off the escalator. The step you were standing on folds down and slides under the floor. It moves along underneath the escalator until it pops up where it started. Then someone else steps on.

Riding the escalator makes life easier for shoppers. You can see that a strong motor turns the gears that pull the stairs up for these passengers. You should always be careful on an escalator and watch where you're going!

Pedal Power!

Hop on, pedal, and zoom away!

When you push your foot down on a bike pedal, the pedal turns a large front sprocket. The sprocket is a wheel with teeth sticking out of it. The teeth fit into, or "mesh," with the bike chain. The sprocket is called the chainwheel because it "drives" the chain. The chain moves a smaller sprocket on the back wheel. Every time you push on the pedal, the back wheel moves around two or three times.

gear shift

hand brake

seat

brake cable

rear brake

front brake

sprocket

tire

pedal

chainwheel

chain

sprocket wheel

50

The larger the sprocket, the lower the gear. The smaller the sprocket, the higher the gear. A low gear makes it easier to pedal. It is used for pedaling uphill or against the wind.

Some bikes have many gears. A high gear lets you pedal slowly but move the bike a long way.

high gear speed

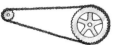

low gear speed

recumbent bike

Imagine pedaling a bike while you sit in a chair with your legs straight out in front of you. This is how you ride a recumbent (rih KUHM behnt) bike. Some recumbent bikes have no handlebars. You steer with levers beneath the seat.

Uni means "one." A unicycle has only one wheel. It takes great balance to ride a unicycle. You need to keep yourself steady, seated above the wheel. But you also need to steer using the pedals and leaning your body slightly to the left or right.

unicycle

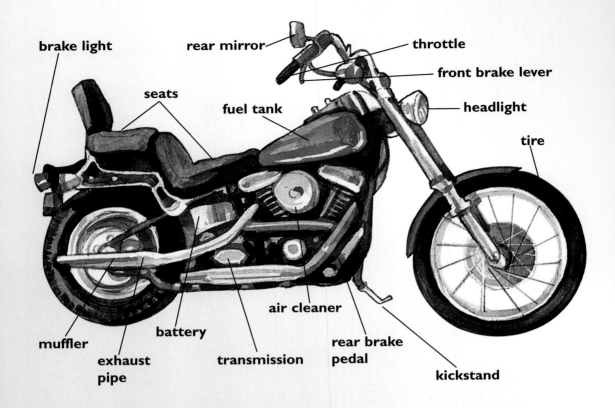

brake light

rear mirror

throttle

front brake lever

seats

fuel tank

headlight

tire

air cleaner

muffler

battery

exhaust pipe

transmission

rear brake pedal

kickstand

A motorcycle is partly like a bike. It has a small seat, handlebars, and a bike stand. But a motorcycle is also partly like a car. It has an engine, a gas tank, an exhaust pipe, headlights, and brake lights.

Motorcycles

Motorcycles are like bicycles with an engine but the frame is much stronger to hold the engine in place.

Most motorcycles are cheaper to buy and run than cars. They use less gasoline and make less pollution. They are popular in countries with heavy traffic or expensive gasoline. Europe, East Asia, and South America have more motorcycles than cars.

Riders drive their motorcycles with foot and hand controls. Twisting the right handlebar controls the speed. A lever on the left handlebar shifts the engine gears like shifting gears on a bike. The motorcycle is slowed by using two brakes. The rider controls the brakes using both his hands and his feet. The front brake is controlled by a lever on the left handlebar. The back brake is controlled by a foot pedal.

Motorcycle riders help steer and control the motorcycle with their bodies, just as you do with a bicycle.

Motorcyclists, or bikers, wear heavy jackets to avoid injury if they fall off. Strong helmets protect their heads.

Motorcycles have improved a lot from this first model, developed by Gottlieb Daimler in 1885. He added an engine to a bicycle.

Motor Moving

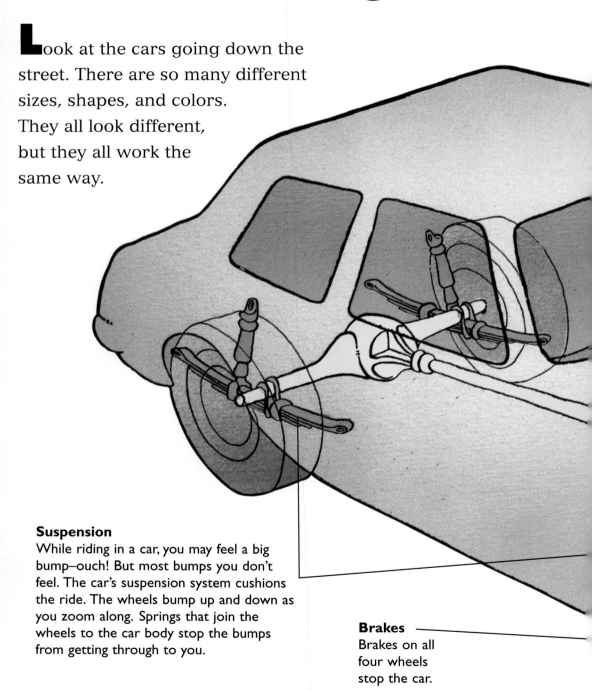

Look at the cars going down the street. There are so many different sizes, shapes, and colors. They all look different, but they all work the same way.

Suspension
While riding in a car, you may feel a big bump—ouch! But most bumps you don't feel. The car's suspension system cushions the ride. The wheels bump up and down as you zoom along. Springs that join the wheels to the car body stop the bumps from getting through to you.

Brakes
Brakes on all four wheels stop the car.

Steering wheel
The steering wheel controls the front wheels. A driver turns the steering wheel to make turns and follow bends in the road.

Gearshift
In many other cars, the transmission changes the gears as the speed of the car increases. In some cars, the driver uses a clutch pedal and a gearshift to change gears.

Engine
The engine makes the power, so the car can move.

Generator
The engine turns the generator, which makes electricity to run the lights and other electric parts.

Transmission
The transmission connects the engine to the wheels. Gears in the transmission control how fast the engine turns the wheels.

Piston Pumper

Dad turns the key in the ignition and the car engine roars to life. What is happening?

Turning the ignition sends power from the battery to the starter motor. The starter motor moves the pistons. As the

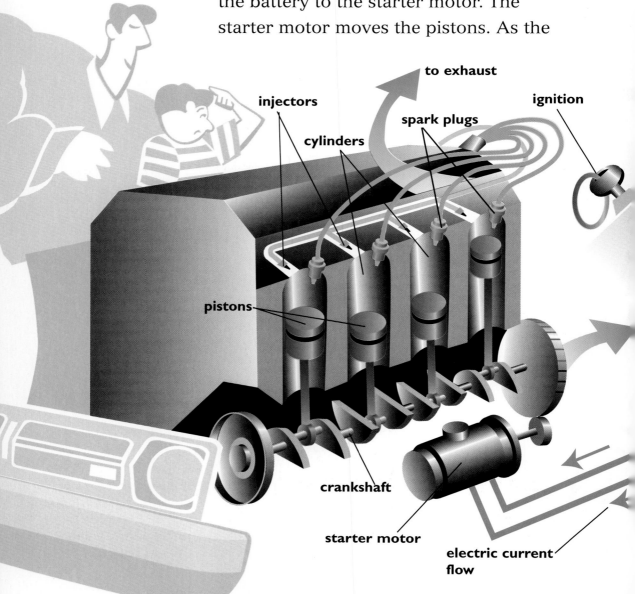

injectors

cylinders

to exhaust

spark plugs

ignition

pistons

crankshaft

starter motor

electric current flow

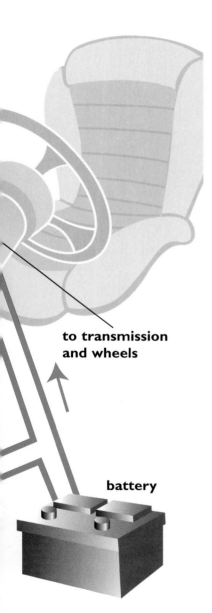

to transmission and wheels

battery

pistons move down, they pull air and gasoline into the cylinders.

Injectors spray fuel into the cylinders. The spark plugs send an electric spark to the cylinders. This spark makes the mixture burn. As it burns, it turns into hot **gases**. The gases expand, or spread out, causing tiny explosions.

These explosions push against the pistons, the pistons push down against a bar called a crankshaft. The crankshaft turns. As it turns, it provides power that makes the wheels turn.

As the pistons push up again, they force the burned gases out of the cylinder. The burned gases flow through the muffler and tailpipe into the air.

Truckin'

TRY THIS!
1

Today, nearly everything we eat, wear, or use is brought to us by a truck. Because trucks do so many kinds of work, there are many kinds of trucks. Which truck should carry each thing shown?

See pages 180-181 for answers.

A

B

C

family

mail

a car that won't run

furniture

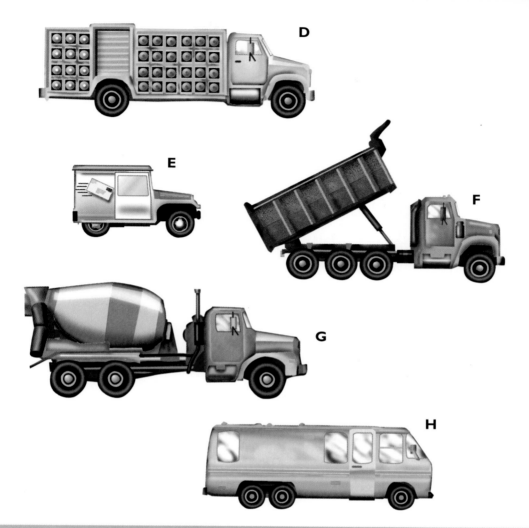

D

E

F

G

H

bottled water

garbage

dirt

wet concrete

Freight trains carry goods and supplies over long distances. This freight train is traveling through Banff National Park in Canada.

Traveling by Track

People all over the world use trains. There are many different kinds of trains. Some trains pull cars filled with goods. Cattle, oil, coal, and automobiles are transported in special types of cars. Trains also carry semitrailers and containers for ships.

Trains that carry people are called passenger trains. Passenger trains have washrooms. They sometimes have a dining car so that passengers can eat. Some even have sleeping cars.

Some passenger trains make short trips. Many people travel to work in trains. Most of these trains are very fast. Great Britain has one of the world's fastest intercity (between cities) trains.

Tracks keep the train on its path. The motor turns the wheels. The wheels turn on tracks. Most tracks are made of two rails, but some use only one rail.

Trains have many cars linked together. The engine car provides the power. It is

Some trains have dining cars. These passengers enjoy their meals on the American Orient Express train in the southwest United States.

Few steam engines are still in use. This steam train, part of Strasburg Rail Road, is the oldest shortline train in the United States.

Trolleys, also called street cars, are common sights in some cities. This Old Town Tram runs in Prague, a city in the Czech Republic.

usually the front car, but an engine can pull or push a train, so sometimes it is the last car. Trains are powered by steam, diesel fuel, or electricity. Few steam engines are used today. Modern

Subways run regular routes at set times all day long. These people wait for the next subway train in an underground station in Washington, D.C.

locomotives are faster and cleaner than steam engines. They use less fuel, too.

Trolley cars are trains that look like buses. They have one car that holds many passengers. Their metal wheels run on two rails in the street. A cable hangs above the rails. It supplies electric power for the trolley.

Subway trains move on tracks underground. They also have a third rail. The third rail provides electric power to make the car move.

Why Things Float

Have you ever noticed how the water in the bathtub rises when you get in? This happens because your body weight pushes the water aside, or displaces it.

What happens when you get into a larger body of water? You'll float! Your body pushes aside enough water to equal your weight. But the water also pushes back against your body, so you float! This is called **buoyancy** (BOY uhn see). Buoyancy is the upward push of displaced water.

If you could weigh the water your body displaced, it would be equal to the **pressure** (PREHSH uhr) of

The pressure of water pushing up on your body makes you float, the same way it makes these ships float, *top*.

the water pushing up on your body. The pressure pushing up cancels out your weight pushing down.

So why do some objects sink? Objects that are heavier than the same amount of water sink in water. When you throw a rock into the water, it weighs more than the amount of water it displaces, so it sinks.

On dry land, this ship weighs 50,000 tons.

In the water, the ship floats.

This is because the ship has pushed away 50,000 tons of water—the same weight as the ship.

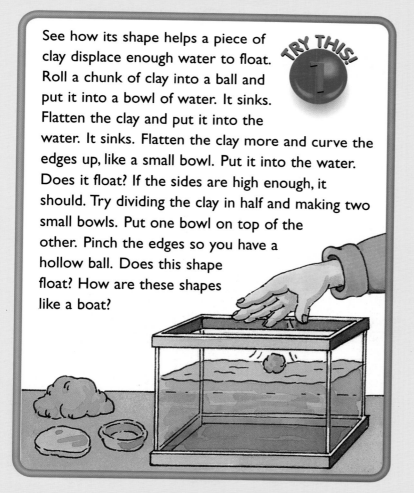

TRY THIS!
1

See how its shape helps a piece of clay displace enough water to float. Roll a chunk of clay into a ball and put it into a bowl of water. It sinks. Flatten the clay and put it into the water. It sinks. Flatten the clay more and curve the edges up, like a small bowl. Put it into the water. Does it float? If the sides are high enough, it should. Try dividing the clay in half and making two small bowls. Put one bowl on top of the other. Pinch the edges so you have a hollow ball. Does this shape float? How are these shapes like a boat?

Make a Magnet Raft

Create your own boat with a few supplies found around the house. Most real boats use sails or motors to make them move across the water, but you can move your boat around a bowl of water using a magnet.

You Will Need:

a horseshoe or bar
  magnet
a large needle
pins
a plastic lid (from a
  margarine tub or
  coffee can)
a small square of paper
  decorated as a sail
a large bowl of water

What To Do:

1. Choose the magnet pole you will use. Use only one pole—north or south. Ask an adult to stroke the end of the magnet down the length of the needle 50 times from the eye to the point. Always rub in the same direction.

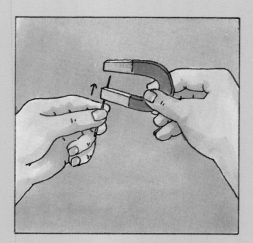

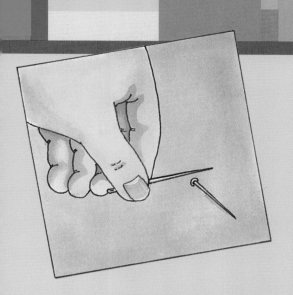

2. Test the needle to see if it now has a magnetic pull. Will it pick up a pin? Be very careful since you are using pins and needles.

3. Have an adult rub the needle 50 more times with the magnet. Make sure you use the same pole. Pin the magnetic needle through the paper sail.

4. Fasten the sail in the center of the plastic lid. Float the raft in the bowl of water. Use the different poles of the magnet to push and pull the raft around the water.

Modern Ships

A ship is a big boat. Ships are designed to travel the ocean. They usually have several decks, or floors, below the water level.

Some ships, like cruise liners, are out at sea for a long time. They have places for sleeping, eating, working, relaxing, and bathing. A luxury cruise liner even has a hospital, hair salon, shops, and swimming pools.

Most ships are working ships. They are used to carry goods or cargo.

Big ships need smaller workboats, tugboats, *above*, to pull or push them away from the dock and into open water. Once in open water, large ships, like this tanker, *below*, can power up and head out to sea.

Planes and helicopters cover the deck of this aircraft carrier. The planes are moved to the runway, the white stripes down the center, when ready for flight.

Freighters carry bananas, cotton, coffee, plastics, and cloth. The cargo travels in big metal boxes. Tankers carry bulk cargo, like crude oil or wheat. The cargo is poured right into the hull.

Some fishing ships are like floating factories. They process and freeze the fish on board the ship. Sometimes these ships are at sea for months.

Some Navy ships have large upper decks. Fighter jets land and take off from this deck. Some Navy ships carry researchers, soldiers, tanks, and even helicopters.

Submarines

Submarines are vessels that can travel underwater. They can also float on the surface of the sea and move like any other ship.

Many submarines are powered by a nuclear reactor. The nuclear reactor creates extreme heat used to turn water into steam. The steam drives an engine that turns the propeller. The propeller pushes the submarine through the water.

Tanks on the sides of the submarine are filled with air or water. They allow the submarine to dive or surface. Doors, called vents, on the top and bottom of each tank, open and close, letting in water or air.

While the submarine is on the surface, the tanks are filled with air. To dive, the vents are opened.

To make the sub surface, the bottom vents are opened. The top vents remain shut. Air is pumped into the tanks to blow out the water. When the sub reaches the surface again, all the vents are shut.

While at the surface, special doors called vents are shut on tanks full of air.

In 1960, the Triton traveled around the world underwater. It took 84 days.

KNOW It All!

70

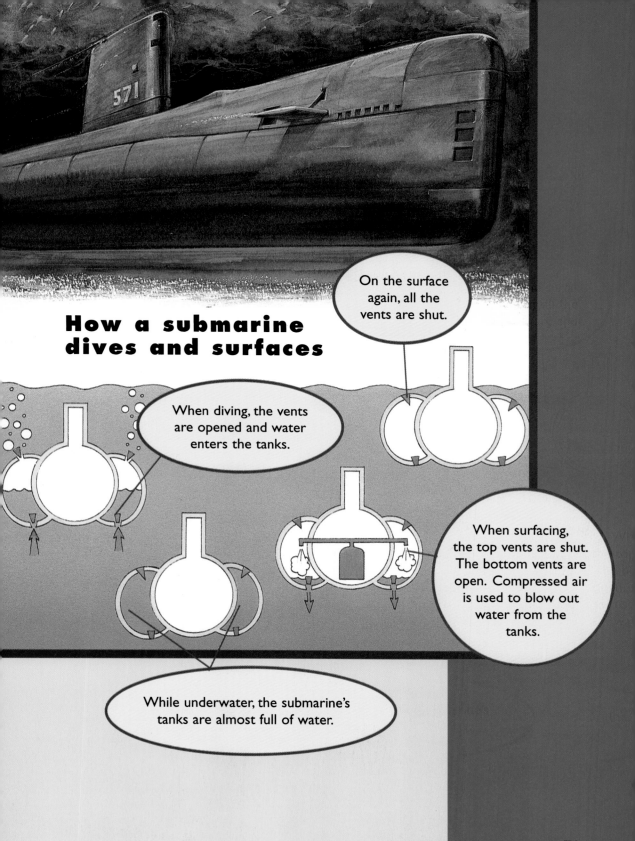

How a submarine dives and surfaces

On the surface again, all the vents are shut.

When diving, the vents are opened and water enters the tanks.

When surfacing, the top vents are shut. The bottom vents are open. Compressed air is used to blow out water from the tanks.

While underwater, the submarine's tanks are almost full of water.

Whirlybird

1. helicopter on the ground

The helicopter pilot starts the engine. Its big blades spin–slowly at first, then faster and faster. But the helicopter is still on the ground. The pilot twists the big blades at an angle. This forces air down. Then the helicopter rises off the ground. The pilot tilts the blades back. The helicopter stops rising and moves forward. A small propeller

2. blades tilting at an angle for take-off

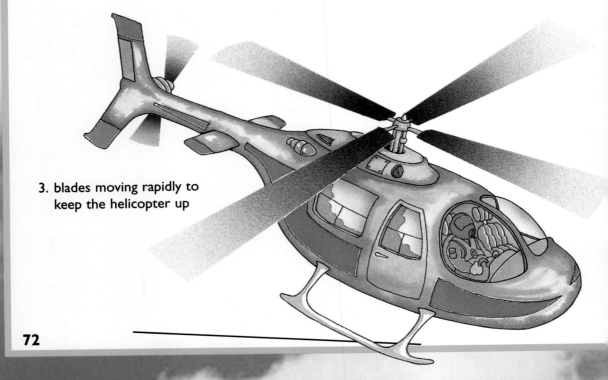

3. blades moving rapidly to keep the helicopter up

at the back of the helicopter keeps it from spinning while the big blades are turning. It also keeps the helicopter from spinning around when it is in the air.

Helicopters are very useful. Since they rise straight into the air, they can land and take off in very small spaces. They can also hover (HUH vuhr), or stay in one place. So they are often used to help people who are trapped on a mountain, at sea, or on top of a high building.

This rescue helicopter hovers above a floating ice pack. It lowers a long, flat basket and hoists stranded campers up one by one.

Jets

This L1011 Tristan passenger jet has just taken off. Two turbine engines give this jet plenty of power.

Airplanes are usually pushed through the air either by propellers or by jet engines. A propeller looks like two thin, pointed wings joined end to end. As it spins around, it forces air backward. This pushes the airplane forward.

The engine of a propeller plane uses the power of burning fuel to turn the propeller. But a jet engine uses burning fuel to make the wheels of a **turbine** (TUHR byn) spin. The gases and air from the spinning turbines shoot out the back of the engine and push the plane forward. An airplane with a jet engine can fly much faster than a propeller airplane.

Large passenger airplanes are usually powered by jet engines. Some jumbo jets can carry more than 400 people. They fly at a speed of 500 to 600 miles (800 to 970 kilometers) an hour.

The Concorde is the fastest passenger plane. It flies about 1,560 miles (2,500 kilometers) an hour. It uses huge amounts of fuel, so it is expensive to run. It is also very noisy.

See How a Turbine Blade Spins

A turbine blade is similar to the blades on an electric fan. The angled blades draw air from behind and pull it forward. This activity will show you how the angled blades help the turbine spin.

You Will Need:

scissors
a piece of cardboard
a pencil

1. Cut a 6-inch (15-cm) circle out of the cardboard. Using a pencil or the point of the scissors, carefully poke a 1/4-inch (1/2-cm) hole in the center.

2. Draw a circle around the hole about 1/4 inch (1/2 cm) outside it.

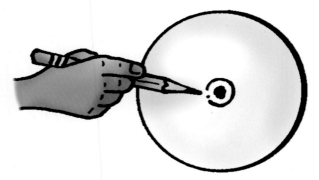

3. Make 8 slits, evenly spaced around the circle. Cut from the edge to the 1/4-inch (1/2-cm) mark. Do not cut all the way through. These are the blades.

4. Bend one side of each blade in the same direction.

5. Put the pencil through the hole.

6. Holding each end of the pencil, place the turbine about 8 inches (20 cm) from your body.

7. Blow on the turbine. How fast can you make it spin?

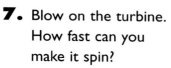

The turbine on a jet engine is similar, but it has two or three times as many blades.

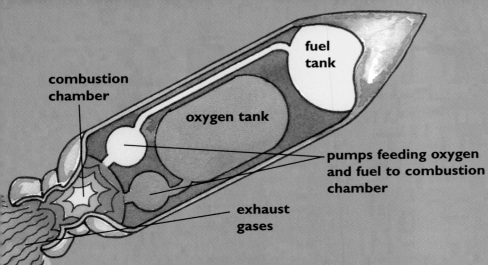

fuel tank

combustion chamber

oxygen tank

pumps feeding oxygen and fuel to combustion chamber

exhaust gases

Rockets

A jet fighter plane is very powerful, but it can't fly into space. Why not? There is no oxygen in space to power the engine!

All fuel needs oxygen to burn, but a rocket engine does not need air. It carries its own supply of oxygen.

Planes get oxygen from the air. But rockets get oxygen from a substance called an **oxidizer** (AHK suh DY zuhr). Some space rockets use solid fuels with solid oxidizers. They work in the same way as a fireworks rocket—a fireworks rocket as big as a 10-story building!

Other space rockets use liquid fuels and oxidizers, so that the engines can be switched on or off.

A Delta rocket launches a NASA satellite.

The liquids are pumped into a special part of the rocket called the **combustion** (kuhm BUHS chuhn) chamber. Here the fuel burns violently to thrust the rocket upwards.

The Saturn V moon rocket burned over 560,000 gallons (2,120,000 liters) of fuel during its first 105 seconds of flight. This pushed the rocket off the launching pad with a huge amount of force. If you want to get to the moon and back again you have to think big—really big!

Fireworks rockets are displayed at many festivals. Fuel in a fireworks rocket burns like fuel in a rocket engine. In fireworks, the fuel is charcoal and sulfur. The oxygen is supplied by a solid oxidizer called saltpeter. This mixture burns very hot. The gases given off push in all directions against the inside of the rocket. The gases that push against the top of the rocket make the rocket go! The fireworks rocket has a stick that keeps it pointed in the right direction.

KNOW It All!

What Makes It Fly?

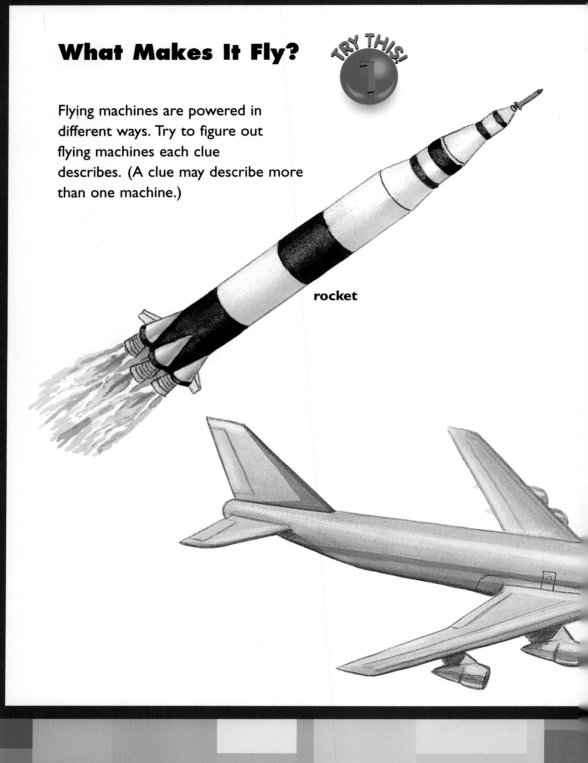

Flying machines are powered in different ways. Try to figure out flying machines each clue describes. (A clue may describe more than one machine.)

rocket

propeller plane

1. Its spinning wings can be tilted to make it go up, or down, or hover (stay in one place).

2. It carries its own oxygen to burn with the fuel.

3. Spinning parts outside its body make it move.

4. Spinning blades make it move forward, but it can't hover.

5. Air flowing over its fixed wings helps it lift.

6. The curved shape of its fixed wings improves its lift.

7. It travels fast enough to break the pull of gravity.

8. It must tilt up in front to fly backward.

9. The fuel burns fiercely and gases push upward to give it lift.

10. Its engines help it move fast by pushing out air and gas at high speed.

jet plane

helicopter

See page 181 for answers.

Who Designs Cars?

Many people work together to design a new car.

First, drawings are made with a computer. This is called computer-aided design, or CAD. Computers are used to create, test, and change the plans. This saves time and money.

Top, car designers look over a computer version of a car design. They can make changes and see what the new design will look like before the car is built. *Bottom*, a clay model is made of the new car design before parts are made for assembly. Adjustments can still be made to the final design at this stage.

Next, artists may make a clay model of the car. The clay is coated with shiny film. It looks like a real car.

Other artists create the inside of the car. They design the seats. They decide where the controls will be. They plan everything from turn signals and seat belts to airbags and drink holders.

Finally, a fiberglass model of the car is built. It has real tires, glass windows, and trim. This final model looks exactly like the new car will look.

Product engineers plan how each part of the car will be made. They use a computer that traces every line and curve on the final model. Factories make the parts and a completed car is made and tested.

Next, parts are shipped to several factories to be assembled. Each worker in the **assembly line** (uh SEHM blee lyn) adds a different part. At the end, a complete car rolls off the line.

On this car assembly line, doors are left off so workers can easily and quickly add parts to the inside of the car.

Final touches are put on the cars before they roll off the assembly line as finished vehicles.

Signals in the Air

Throw a stone in a puddle or a lake. Do you see ripples? These ripples are little waves. The ripples expand across the water. Sounds make waves, too. We can't see sound waves or feel them, but we can hear them.

Machines help us hear sounds sent from far away. They receive sound waves as signals, then turn the signals back into sounds we can hear.

Radios, televisions, pagers, remote controls, and security systems all use signals. The air is full of signals. Just imagine if we could see them all!

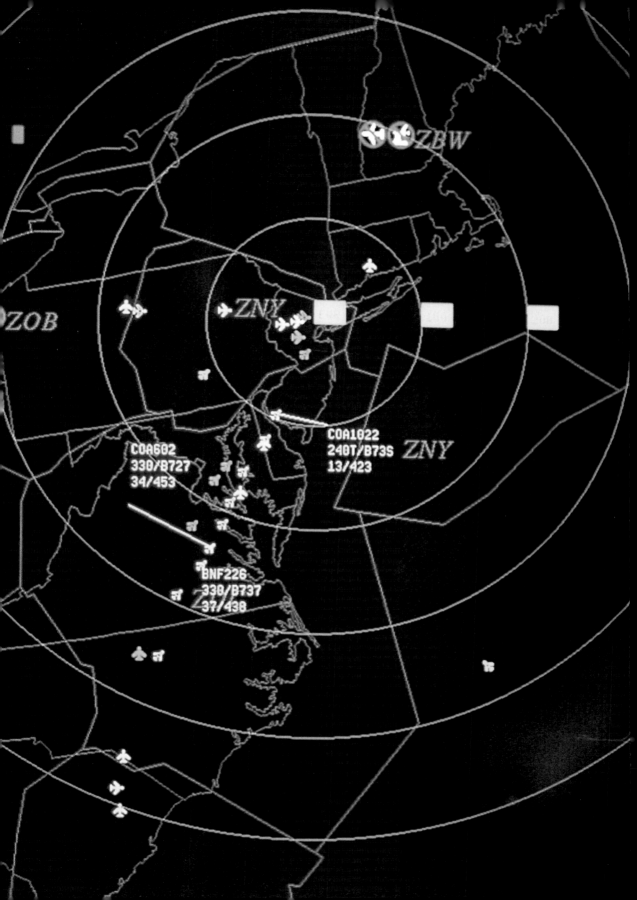

Radios

Radio signals are heard almost everywhere. But how does a radio work?

The radio transmitter changes sound waves into electrical signals. It sends them through the air as **radio waves** (RAY dee oh wayvz). The radio waves that leave the transmitter have different **frequencies** (FREE kwuhn seez) for each station. Frequencies are the number of times the waves vibrate per second.

You tune your radio by choosing a number on the controls. Each number represents a frequency. So if you always tune in the same frequency, you always pick up the same station.

When you tune in a station, signals are picked up by the radio. These signals are sent to an electromagnet in the radio speaker. The electromagnet makes a cone on the speaker vibrate. These vibrations are the sounds you hear on your radio. They sound exactly like the sounds made at the transmitter—voices, music, or even the squeak of a mouse.

Guglielmo Marconi

Two young women listen to the radio using headphones. With headphones, you can listen to your portable radio outside or inside.

Television

Did you know that the pictures on TV are a jumble of red, green, and blue dots? When you sit across the room, the dots blend into the images you see.

At the television station, a camera records the picture and sound from the scene you are watching. Mirrors in the camera split light from the scene into red, green, and blue. A tube in the camera changes the light to radio signals. The television station broadcasts the program to your home.

A TV antenna, cable, or satellite dish receives many broadcast signals at once. The television tuner is used to select the signal for the TV channel you want to see. The tuner passes this signal to the amplifier. The amplifier separates the sound from the pictures.

The sound goes to the speakers. The picture signal is sent to a decoder. The decoder sends the signal to the electron guns. There is one gun for each color— red, blue, and green. The electron guns zip across the screen in weak or strong bursts of light. These bursts form the picture you see on the screen.

Cable stations send electrical signals along underground wires to your home.

Pixel Play

Screens in TVs and computers have millions of tiny dots or squares, called pixels (PIK zuhlz). This activity will show you how the three colors—red, blue, and green—combine to make images you see on a TV or computer screen.

You Will Need:

2 sheets of graph paper
   with very small grids
a red marker or crayon
a green marker or crayon
a blue marker or crayon

What To Do:

1. Using graph paper, color each square in a row with a different color marker. Color one square red, one square green, one square blue, and so on.

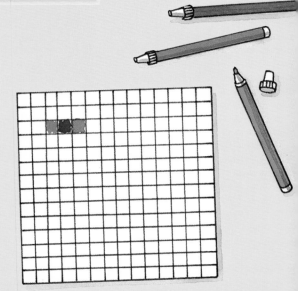

2. In another row, color 3 or more squares green, the next 3 squares red, and the next 3 squares blue. Have someone hold the graph paper across the room from you. What do you see? Do the colors seem to blend?

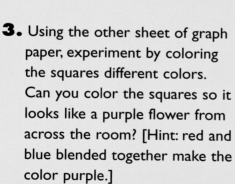

3. Using the other sheet of graph paper, experiment by coloring the squares different colors. Can you color the squares so it looks like a purple flower from across the room? [Hint: red and blue blended together make the color purple.]

How Does a Remote Control Work?

Have you ever tried to switch channels on TV when someone stood in the way? Nothing happened. Why not? The transmission of the signal was blocked. The signal from the remote control hit someone's body instead of the TV.

Remote means "far away." When you use the remote control, you are controlling the TV from a distance. The remote uses an invisible type of light

called **infrared** (ihn fruh REHD) light to send a signal to a receiver on the TV.

The buttons on your remote control send different codes to the TV. The code consists of long and short flashes of infrared light. When you press a button, the remote control sends the code for that button to the receiver in the TV. The TV "sees" the signal and carries out the command.

KNOW It All!

Some toy cars use a radio remote control to guide their movements. Turning knobs or moving levers sends a signal to the car to go forward or backward, or turn left or right. A garage-door opener uses a radio wave to send its signal. Different openers have different frequencies so that you won't open your neighbor's garage door by mistake.

Tracking Signals

Airplanes get into traffic jams just as cars do—especially around busy airports. But people called air traffic controllers know where each plane is located. They use **radar** (RAY dahr) to help them direct air traffic.

Radar allows the controllers to find planes that are too far away to see. And radar does this at night and in rain, fog, or snow.

A radar set sends out radio waves. When the radio waves hit a flying plane, or even a raindrop, they bounce back to the radar set. This makes spots of light appear on the tracking screen.

The moving spots of light tell a controller where the object is. They know how far away it is, how high it is, how fast it is moving, and which way it is going. Then the controllers can direct the air traffic, much as police officers direct road traffic. They make sure each plane follows a safe path when flying, taking off, or landing.

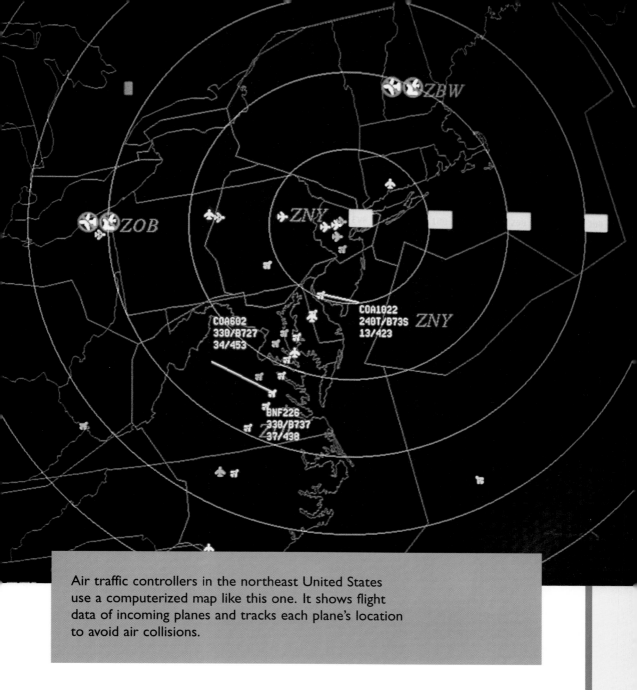

COA1022
240T/B73S ZNY
13/423

COA602
330/B727
34/453

BNF226
330/B737
37/438

ZBW

ZOB

ZNY

Air traffic controllers in the northeast United States use a computerized map like this one. It shows flight data of incoming planes and tracks each plane's location to avoid air collisions.

The planes have radar sets, too. The pilot can look at the radar to make sure that no violent storms or other planes are dangerously close.

Safe Signals

A store owner is closing up shop for the night. Before leaving, the owner sets the security alarm by punching a code into a keypad.

Many people use security systems to stay safe. Security systems use signals that tell them when to sound the alarm. Codes are entered in a keypad near the door. This turns the system on and off. If you forget to turn off the alarm when you return, the alarm will sound.

A small transmitter inside this building sends radar waves scattering and bouncing around the room, setting up an invisible pattern.

Security signals keep us safe in many ways. Airports and courthouses use metal detectors to detect weapons. Many look like doorways. A transmitter on each side of the doorway sends out radio waves. Metal absorbs some of these waves and reflects them, or sends them back. The detector's transmitter then beeps, or signals that metal is there.

Libraries and stores prevent theft by placing coded targets on items. The target sets off an alarm at the exit if it has not gone through the check-out process.

GATES B·C·D

Many security systems use a motion alarm. A small transmitter inside the house sends radar waves into the room. The waves scatter and bounce around the room. They set up an invisible pattern. When someone enters the room, the pattern is upset, and the alarm goes off. A motion alarm will not work well if you have pets. When the pets move, they set off the alarm.

Another type of security system uses metal strips on the windows. When the window is closed, the metal strips touch each other. When the window is opened, this connection is broken and an alarm goes off.

Faster Signal Lines

Pick up your telephone and call a friend. As you punch the buttons, signals travel on the phone line to your local telephone center. That center sends the signals to the phone center nearest your friend.

While you are calling your friend, thousands of other people are making calls, too! And some people are using modems. Modems are machines that send information from one computer to another over phone lines. Other people use fax machines or e-mail to send letters over phone lines. Today, people are sending out more messages than ever, and phone lines help

us to communicate across the world!

Microwave (MY kroh wayv) links and optical fibers can

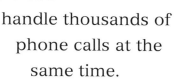

handle thousands of phone calls at the same time. Microwave links send signals as a radio beam. At the receiving station, the microwave signals are decoded.

Optical fibers are long strands of coated glass. Optical fiber cables can carry thousands of telephone conversations and faxes, as well as computer information. They carry television programs, too. Lasers are used to turn the messages into pulses of light. The light pulses are then decoded at the other end of the optical fiber.

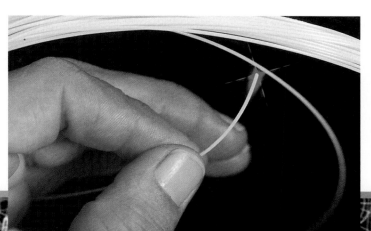

Optical fiber cables carry telephone conversations, faxes, computer information, and television programs.

Give Me a Ring

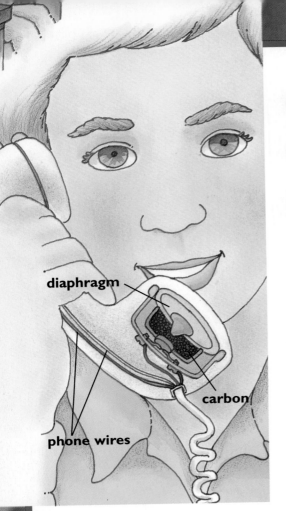

diaphragm

carbon

phone wires

When you call your friend on the phone, how does your voice reach them? You speak into the mouthpiece of your phone. The sound waves push on a thin sheet of metal called a **diaphragm** (DY uh frahm).

The diaphragm then **vibrates** (VY brayts). It presses against a small cup filled with **carbon** (KAHR buhn) grains.

Electricity passes through the carbon on its way through the telephone wire. When the carbon grains are squeezed together, the electric current gets through easily. But when the grains are spread apart, only a little current gets through. So the vibrating diaphragm causes strong or weak

KNOW It All!!

The first telephone was not like our phones today. You could speak into it but you could not hear the other person on it. Alexander Graham Bell first used it in March 1876. But by October of that year, Bell had the first two-way conversation on his invention.

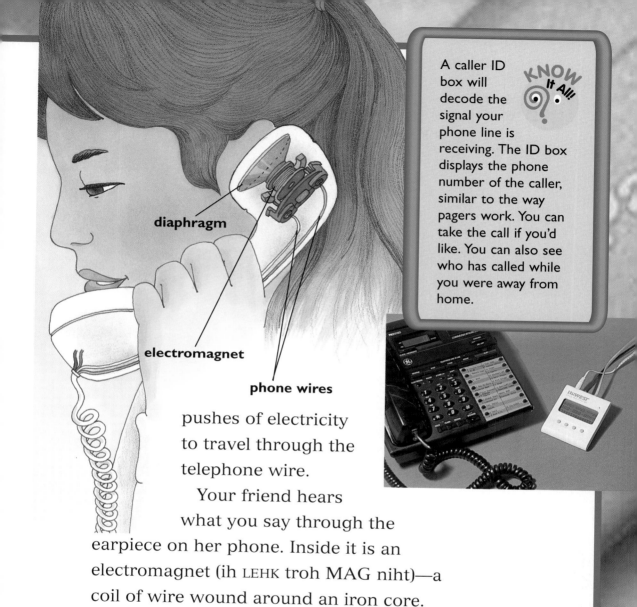

diaphragm

electromagnet

phone wires

A caller ID box will decode the signal your phone line is receiving. The ID box displays the phone number of the caller, similar to the way pagers work. You can take the call if you'd like. You can also see who has called while you were away from home.

KNOW It All!

pushes of electricity to travel through the telephone wire.

Your friend hears what you say through the earpiece on her phone. Inside it is an electromagnet (ih LEHK troh MAG niht)—a coil of wire wound around an iron core. The strong or weak pushes of electricity reach the electromagnet. They cause it to make strong or weak pulls on another diaphragm. This diaphragm vibrates and makes sounds just like the ones you made. So your friend hears a copy of your voice— a copy made by electricity in a wire.

Communicating on the Go!

Beep! Beep! Beep! What was that noise? You're inside a building, so it's not a car horn. It came from a small box on someone's belt—a pager. The beep means that person has a message or a call from someone.

A pager, or beeper, beeps or vibrates when it receives a signal. A display shows the phone number of the caller and possibly a message, too!

Some people also carry phones in their purses, briefcases, or cars. Many of these are cellular phones, or cell phones. Both cellular phones and pagers use radio signals to carry their messages.

The service area for cell phones and pagers is divided into groups called cells. Each cell has a radio transmitter. Signals are sent to the cell where the person using the pager or cell phone is. People who move around a lot still get their signals. The signals bounce from the

transmitter in one cell to the transmitter in the next cell. This happens very quickly. Even if people are in their car while they are talking on the cell phone, their conversation is not interrupted.

When you call a friend from a cell phone, the signal goes through many connections before it reaches your friend.

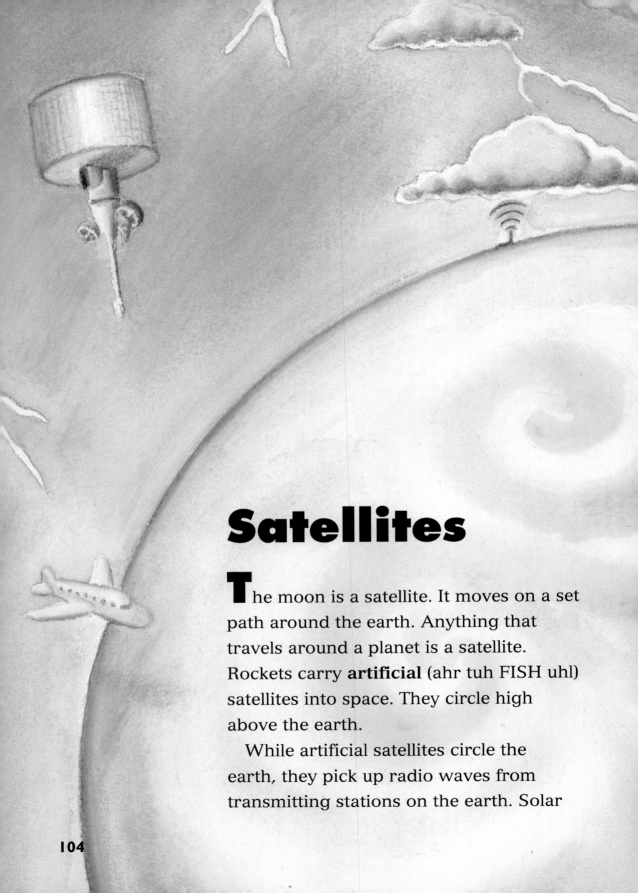

Satellites

The moon is a satellite. It moves on a set path around the earth. Anything that travels around a planet is a satellite. Rockets carry **artificial** (ahr tuh FISH uhl) satellites into space. They circle high above the earth.

While artificial satellites circle the earth, they pick up radio waves from transmitting stations on the earth. Solar

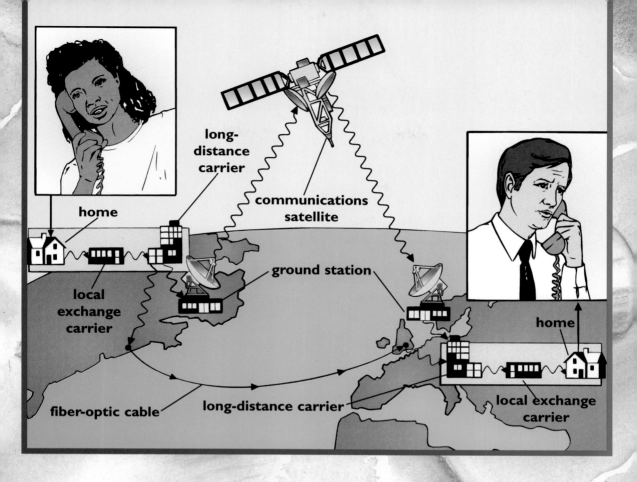

long-distance carrier

communications satellite

home

ground station

local exchange carrier

fiber-optic cable

long-distance carrier

home

local exchange carrier

panels on the satellites collect sunlight to make electricity. They use this electricity to send the radio waves back to receiving stations. The receiving stations are often thousands of miles away from the transmitting station.

Today, many hundreds of satellites whirl around the earth. Each one makes life easier for people on the ground.

The Internet

The Internet is a network of computers around the world. A network of computers means each computer is linked or connected. The Internet allows people in different cities, and even different countries, to share information from one computer to another.

Think of a map used for traveling by car. It is a network of lines that connect and cross. The Internet is similar, except you cannot see all the phone lines, cables, and connections that the information travels through to reach your computer.

To connect to the Internet, your computer needs a modem (MOH duhm). This device connects the computer to a phone line and, with the help of a computer program, translates information from the computer into a digital code. The code is sent through phone lines and satellites in small pieces called packets. The packets may be sent along different routes so they reach another computer as quickly as possible.

Networks may be big or small. Small networks, called local area networks, or LANs, connect computers in one office, school, or building. Wide area networks, or WANs, link computers over larger distances. These computers send information to each other via modems and telephone lines.

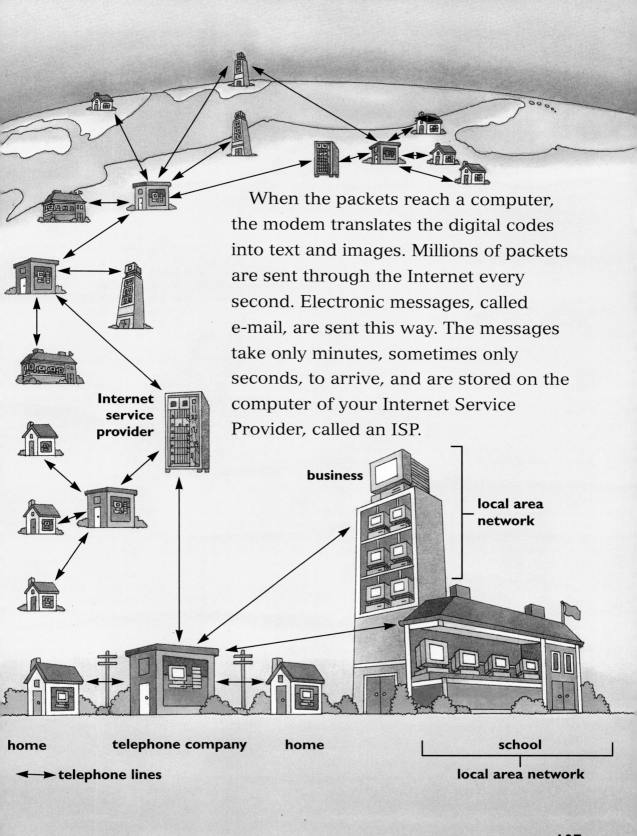

When the packets reach a computer, the modem translates the digital codes into text and images. Millions of packets are sent through the Internet every second. Electronic messages, called e-mail, are sent this way. The messages take only minutes, sometimes only seconds, to arrive, and are stored on the computer of your Internet Service Provider, called an ISP.

Internet service provider

business

local area network

home   telephone company   home   school

◄──► telephone lines   local area network

Does It Send or Receive?

Here are many machines and devices that use signals. Some only receive signals. Some only send signals. Others both receive and send. Can you figure out how the signals work for the following things? For each one, decide if it only receives, only sends, or does both.

See page 181 for answers.

1. clock radio

2. pay telephone

3. microphone

4. garage-door opener

5. walkie-talkie

6. home satellite dish

7. personal stereo

8. cellular phone

9. radio-controlled car

10. pager

11. TV remote control

Raw Materials

Did you know that paper and some medicines come from plants? Did you know plastic bowls, dolls, and action figures began as oil in the middle of the ocean?

Many things people buy began as something else. They began as raw materials. Wood, clay, and sand are raw materials. People have found ways to use these raw materials to make our lives easier. Like the ingredients in many meals, raw materials are combined or processed to make something else that is useful. Read on to find out what raw materials make the things you use!

From the Waterworks

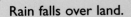

Rain falls over land.

Used water leaves houses through drains. Before reaching rivers, used water is cleaned in sewage works.

Water flows through water mains to faucets in houses.

Thirsty? Turn on the kitchen faucet and fill a glass with water. Where does that water come from? Like other raw materials, water goes to a factory before it reaches your home.

Rain water collects in reservoirs (REHZ urh vwahrz).

Water is filtered in waterworks.

Cleaned water is pumped into water towers.

When it rains, water seeps through the soil and rock. A factory called a waterworks cleans the water for people to use.

First, the waterworks pumps water from underground or a river or lake. Then it filters the water. It removes tiny bits of dirt. The filtered water looks clean, but it may contain germs. Small amounts of chemicals are added to kill the germs.

The treated water flows to a pumping station. The pumping station sends the water to underground pipes called water mains. When you turn on the tap, water comes from the water main into your house.

Some cities pump treated water into water towers. These are called holding tanks. When water is needed, it flows to water mains on your street.

TRY THIS!

Make a Water Filter

You know where drinking water comes from, but where does the dirty water go? Down the sewer. Sewer water is filtered to remove solids before it is pumped into lakes and streams. This activity will help you see how water is filtered in nature and in a processing plant. But you must never drink your filtered water. It may look clean but it could still have germs in it.

You Will Need:

an empty plastic bottle
a small jar with a mouth
   big enough to fit
   around the plastic
   bottle
scissors
cotton balls
muddy water
small, clean pebbles
clean gravel
clean sand

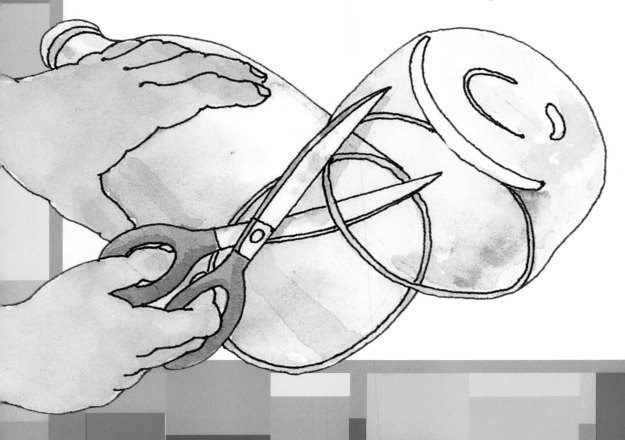

What To Do:

1. Ask an adult to help you cut off the top part of the plastic bottle, about 3 1/2 inches (9 cm) from the cap.

2. Turn the top part of the bottle upside down and place it in the jar.

3. Push a wad of cotton balls into the neck of the bottle. Put in a layer of small pebbles, then a layer of gravel, then a layer of wet sand.

4. Pour some muddy water onto the sand and watch it drip through into the bottom of the bottle.

5. The water that filters through looks cleaner. What happens when you pour the water through the filter a second time? Does it look any cleaner? The water is cleaner, but not completely clean. It is not clean enough to drink. **Do NOT drink it.**

sand

gravel

pebbles

cotton

From Shell to Spread

You can't spread a peanut on your sandwich, but you can spread peanut butter. What happens to peanuts between the field and the lunch table?

First, a machine digs up the peanut plants and shakes off the dirt. Another machine separates the pods, or shells, from the leafy tops. Then the peanuts go to a warehouse, where blowers remove the stems.

Rollers crack open the pods. Inside each pod are one, two, or even three peanut seeds. Another machine gently brushes the skins from seeds. A laser scans for rotten ones.

The remaining seeds are washed and roasted. They go into a grinder with salt, oil, sugar, and other ingredients. The mixture is ground. A conveyor belt moves clean, empty jars along while nozzles squirt peanut butter into the jars. The belt carries the filled jars to the next machine. This machine seals the jars and puts on the caps.

Now the jars are ready to be labeled and shipped.

From Field to Sandwich

A loaf of bread looks nothing like the grains that grow in the field. Making bread from grain takes many steps. Grain needs to be grown, harvested, and ground into flour.

Most bread is made at a bakery. A machine mixes flour, water, yeast, salt, sugar, and oil into a sticky dough. The yeast makes the dough rise, or grow. The dough sits in a warm tank until it doubles in size. Then it moves down a conveyor belt. The dough is cut into pieces and the pieces are shaped into loaves. Then the loaves are dropped into baking pans. A different machine does each step.

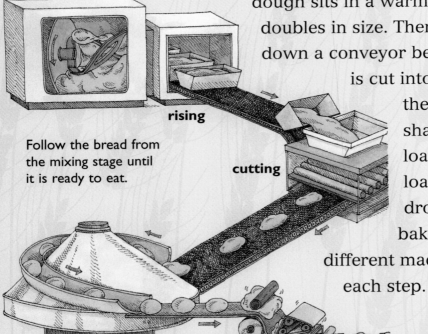

mixing

rising

Follow the bread from the mixing stage until it is ready to eat.

cutting

shaping   **panning**

118

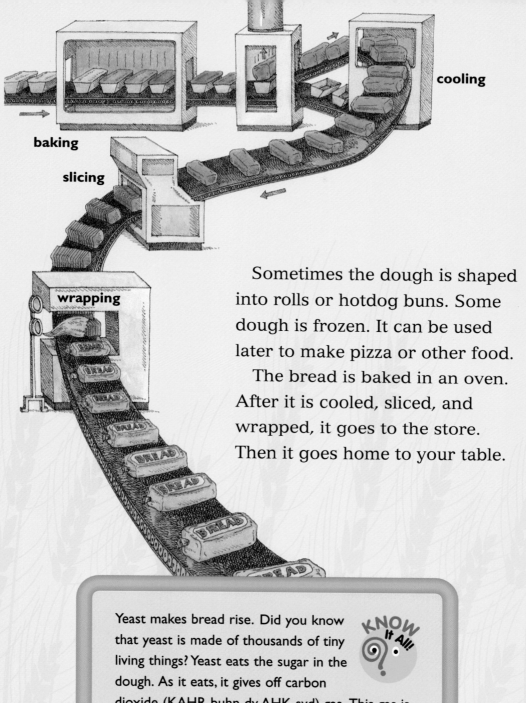

cooling

baking

slicing

wrapping

Sometimes the dough is shaped into rolls or hotdog buns. Some dough is frozen. It can be used later to make pizza or other food.

The bread is baked in an oven. After it is cooled, sliced, and wrapped, it goes to the store. Then it goes home to your table.

KNOW It All!

Yeast makes bread rise. Did you know that yeast is made of thousands of tiny living things? Yeast eats the sugar in the dough. As it eats, it gives off carbon dioxide (KAHR buhn dy AHK syd) gas. This gas is what makes the bubbles in bread dough. When bread is sliced, those bubbles look like tiny holes.

Batter Up!

This bread does not rise very high, but you will see how yeast makes the dough expand. When you slice the bread, you will see the holes made from the gas bubbles.

You Will Need:

1 package active dry yeast (1/4 ounces)
1/4 cup warm water (like bath water, about 110 °F)
1 1/2 cups whole wheat flour
1/2 cup all-purpose flour
1/2 cup rolled oats
1/4 cup packed brown sugar
1 teaspoon salt
2 tablespoons vegetable oil
1 cup very warm water
1 egg
a clean dish towel
a greased bread pan

1. Pour the 1/4 cup (60 ml) *warm* water into a small bowl. Sprinkle in the yeast. It should foam and bubble.

2. In a large bowl, mix the flours, oats, brown sugar, and salt.

3. Add the egg and *very warm* water to the large bowl. Mix.

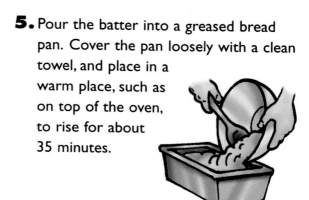

5. Pour the batter into a greased bread pan. Cover the pan loosely with a clean towel, and place in a warm place, such as on top of the oven, to rise for about 35 minutes.

6. Ask an adult to preheat the oven to 200 °F (92 °C) or its lowest setting. Place the bread in the oven for 20 to 30 minutes. It should rise to twice its original height.

4. Pour in the dissolved yeast and stir. The batter should be thick and sticky. Let it rest 20 minutes.

7. Ask an adult to turn up the oven to 350 °F (175 °C). Bake 25 to 30 minutes until lightly browned.

Easy and Cheesy!

Mmm! When it's hot, cheese is stringy and gooey. You know cheese is made with milk. But how does milk get to be cheese?

In a cheese factory, cheese makers pour milk into big tanks. They heat the milk and add something called a "starter" to make the milk turn sour. Next, they add an enzyme (EHN zym) called rennin. The rennin makes the milk thicken and

TRY THIS! 2

Add a couple of spoonfuls of lemon juice and sugar to a half cup of whole milk. Stir. Let it stand for one minute. Now stir again. What happened? Did it get thicker?

Lemon juice is an acid. It sours the milk. But it also reacts with the fats in the milk. The milk thickens, just as it does when making cheese. The sugar speeds up this reaction.

harden. The milk turns into a thick solid called curds (KUHRDZ) and a thin liquid called whey (WAY).

The curds are heated until they are firm and the whey is drained off. Machines salt the curd. It is then cut up and pressed into molds. Most kinds of cheese are stored at a certain temperature for a period of time. This is called aging. Some kinds of cheese are aged for many months to get just the right flavor. When it has aged, the cheese is sent to the store.

KNOW It All!

How was cheese discovered? There is a legend about an Arab traveler accidentally making the first cheese. The legend says that, over 4,000 years ago, this traveler made a trip across the desert. He used a pouch made from a sheep's stomach to carry milk on the trip. Using animal parts like this was common then.

After a long, hot day, the milk turned into a watery, lumpy mixture. Rennin is found in the stomach of some animals. The desert heat and the rennin made the milk separate into curds and whey. Because the traveler was hungry, he ate the curds and whey and found it delicious.

Pizza is a very popular food that has cheese as a main ingredient.

Easy Ice Cream

Did you know milk is also a raw material used in making ice cream? You can make ice cream at home. But you'll need a friend to help shake and roll the mixture.

You Will Need:

a gallon-size zip-top bag
a sandwich or quart-size zip-top bag
newspaper
ice cubes
1 cup whole milk or half-and-half
1 cup coarse salt
1 1/2 tablespoons sugar
1/4 teaspoon vanilla extract or
    1 teaspoon chocolate syrup

1. Pour the milk, sugar, and flavoring into the small zip-top bag. Seal. Squish the bag to mix.

2. Pour the ice and salt into the large zip-top bag.

3. Put the small bag into the large bag. Seal the large bag.

4. Wrap the large bag in newspaper. Roll it so that the ends can be twisted like a candy wrapper. Then twist the ends closed.

5. Now shake the newspaper. Twist and roll it around. After about 20 minutes, check the ice cream. It should be ready to eat. If not, repeat steps 2 to 5 by adding extra ice and salt and shaking again.

Why did the milk turn to ice cream so quickly? Because heat is taken from the ingredients as the salt helps to melt the ice.

Tree-mendous!

Paper is one of the greatest inventions. Imagine a world without it. There would be no books, magazines, newspapers, or boxes. How would we send letters to friends or do homework?

People make paper from trees. The logs go to a paper mill, where the bark is removed. The wood is then chipped into small pieces about the size of your fingernail.

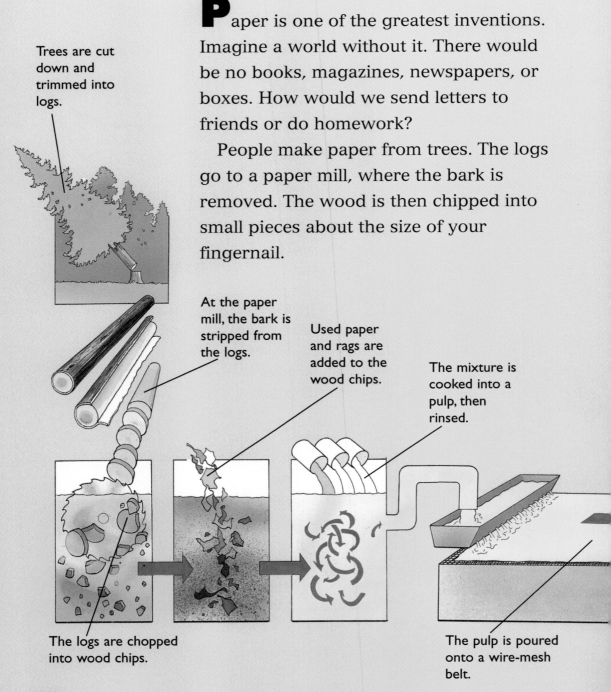

Trees are cut down and trimmed into logs.

At the paper mill, the bark is stripped from the logs.

Used paper and rags are added to the wood chips.

The mixture is cooked into a pulp, then rinsed.

The logs are chopped into wood chips.

The pulp is poured onto a wire-mesh belt.

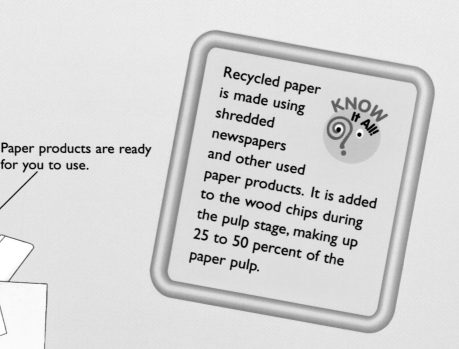

Paper products are ready for you to use.

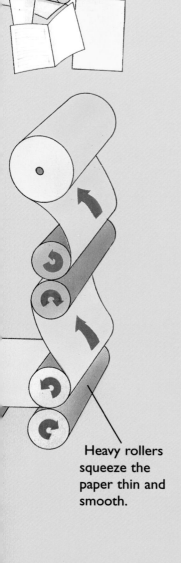

Heavy rollers squeeze the paper thin and smooth.

The wood chips are cooked in steam and chemicals to make a pulp. Sometimes used paper and rags are added. Then the pulp is washed to remove the chemicals and other unwanted materials.

Machines beat the pulp to separate the wood fibers. Sometimes coloring is added at this stage.

Next, the pulp goes to a paper-making machine. It is poured onto a wire-mesh belt that removes the water. After that, rollers squeeze the paper into sheets and dry it.

Finally, the paper goes through heavy rollers that iron it smooth.

Recycle Your Own Paper

TRY THIS! 3

When the Chinese made paper 2,000 years ago, they used garbage. Rags and old fishing nets, along with plants, were boiled in a huge tub of water. They stirred the mixture and beat it into a pulp. They let the water drain and then pressed the pulp. When it dried, it was a sheet of paper. Try making your own!

You Will Need:

used paper or newspaper
leaves and flowers (optional)
2-4 cups (480 ml-960 ml)
    hot water
a bowl
a hand whisk or fork
a baking pan (such as a
    9 x 13 in [23 x 33 cm]
    cake pan)
a rolling pin

newspaper
paper towel
a paper form (a piece of
    wire mesh with folded
    edges or window
    screening in an
    embroidery ring)
an old cloth towel
spray starch

1. Tear the used paper and newspapers into pieces about the size of postage stamps.

2. Drop them into the bowl and add hot water. Beat the mixture until it is smooth. There should be no big pieces left. The pulp should be thick, but thin enough to pour, like a smoothie or slush.

3. Pour the mixture into the baking pan. Then dip the paper form into the pan, sliding it under the mixture. Move the mesh around to get a thick, even layer of mixture on top. You may want to use your fingers to spread the mixture out.

4. Use both hands to lift the paper form straight up out of the pan and let the water drain away. If you like, add a design. Place leaves and flowers on top of the pulp that's on the paper form.

5. Lay the paper form between the pages of a newspaper. Place paper toweling on top of the pulp.

Then roll a rolling pin over the newspaper to blot water from the pulp.

6. Turn the paper form over onto an old cloth towel. Gently remove your homemade paper from the paper form. Let your paper dry on the towel for a day. Spray starch can be used to help "set" the paper and make it easier to write on.

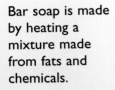
Bar soap is made by heating a mixture made from fats and chemicals.

Cleaning Up

"Wash your hands," your mom says. As you squeeze the liquid soap into your hands, you wonder, "Where's the dirt?" Some flakes of dirt may be too tiny for you to see. But the soap surrounds, "captures," and breaks up the dirt into smaller bits. Once the dirt is broken up, water can rinse it away.

Soap is made by blending animal or vegetable fat and a very strong chemical called lye (LY). Heating this over a hot fire causes a thick, hot liquid to form. Colorings and fragrances are added. Then the mixture is dried.

A machine slices the dried soap into chunks that look like noodles. To make liquid soap, the soap noodles are blended with water and heated again. To make bar soap, the noodles are shaped into "logs" by another machine. These logs are sliced, like a loaf of bread. The "slices" are pressed into shapes and wrapped—bars of soap!

After the soap mixture is dried, it is cut into soap noodles, *left*. The chopped-up soap is shaped into "logs" by another machine, *right*. These logs are cut into the soap bars we use at home.

Clay Creations

What do you think the first storage containers were made of? They may have been made of animal skins or wood or even stone. But around 8,000 B.C., people learned to dig clay from the ground, mold it into a shape, and let the clay dry out until it was hard. The clay containers worked well for storing dry things. But they were not watertight.

The Chinese discovered how to make clay watertight. If clay is heated to a high enough temperature for a long time, it changes chemically. Clay is made of many different minerals. Dirt and mud have some of these minerals, but not enough for the chemical change needed. The chemical changes make

This family makes pottery in the same way people have for many centuries. They live on Cyprus, an island in the Mediterranean Sea.

the clay stronger and watertight. Modern pottery ovens, or kilns, use gas, oil, or electricity to get the heat needed. The temperature must be about 2200 °F (1200 °C) for 14 to 30 hours. This process is called firing.

In modern factories, the clay is shaped by a machine or in a mold. When the clay has been fired, it is ready for glazing. Glazing means covering the clay with a thin layer of liquid glass. The object is then fired again and the result is a clay object covered with shiny glass. It is watertight and ready to use.

Cotton comes from the seed pods of the cotton plant.

Natural Fibers

Look very closely at a piece of thread. Do you see the fibers in it? Fibers are the raw materials of fabric.

Many of our clothes are made of plant fibers. Cotton is the most widely used natural fiber. Its fibers come from the seed pods of the cotton plant. A carding machine makes the tangled strands of cotton all lie in the same direction. Then the strands are twisted and stretched to make cotton thread. When it is woven into cloth, cotton is light and cool to wear.

Linen (LIHN uhn) comes from the stem of the flax plant. After the plants are cut,

Wool comes from sheep.

Linen comes from the flax plant.

they are soaked in water to loosen the fibers in the stems. Machines then clean the fibers and spin them to make linen thread. Linen is woven into very fine cloth. It is cool to wear, even on a hot day.

Silk comes from a caterpillar called a silkworm. It makes silk fibers. It grows by eating leaves from the mulberry tree. Then it spins a cocoon around itself, using one very long strand of fine silk thread. Silk thread is made by twisting the strands of several cocoons together. Pure silk cloth is thin and fine, but very strong.

We get wool from animals. Most wool comes from sheep. The farmers usually shear the sheep once a year. The fibers are straightened to make yarn. Pure wool can be knitted or woven to make warm clothes.

Jute is used for sacks.

Silk is spun by the silkworm.

Machine-created glass objects, like these bottles, *top*, can be as beautiful as those that are hand-blown, *bottom*.

Liquid Sand

The next time you drink your favorite juice, look carefully at the cup. Is it made of glass? Look at the windows in your house. They are made of glass. Marbles are usually made of glass, too. Where does glass come from? Actually, it's mostly sand!

Glass is made by mixing sand with chemicals. The mixture is heated above 2600 °F (1430 °C). Colored glass is made by adding chemicals. To make the sheets of glass you see in windows, liquid glass is poured onto melted tin and pulled onto rollers when it sets.

Glass containers were first made about 4,000 years ago. The liquid glass was built up around a piece of clay. When the glass hardened, the clay was removed. About 2,000 years ago, someone discovered that a gob of liquid glass on the end of a tube could be blown into a hollow shape—like your juice glass!

Today, most glass items are made by machines. Gobs of liquid glass are pushed into molds. Others are formed by people who use fire to heat the glass and make it soft enough to blow.

This glass blower uses a long tube to blow through, so the heat from the glass won't burn him.

Meltdown

Look around you. What objects do you see that are made of metal? The doorknob may be made of iron or brass. Your fork and spoon may be made of steel or silver. The ring on your mom's or dad's finger may be made of gold or silver. Metals are all around us. But where do they come from?

You can't dig metal out of the ground. But the ore, or mineral, that metal comes

A blast furnace separates metal from ore.

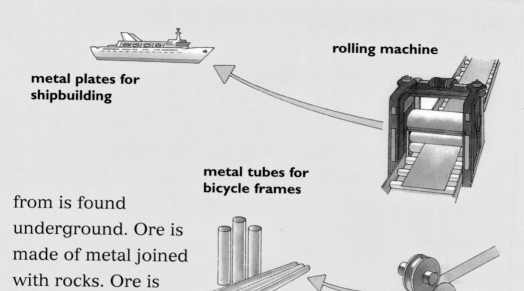

metal plates for shipbuilding

rolling machine

metal tubes for bicycle frames

rolling machine

One type of machine rolls wide, flat shapes. Another kind of rolling machine makes tubes.

from is found underground. Ore is made of metal joined with rocks. Ore is metal in its raw form.

To get metals out of the ground, miners first dig out the ore. The ore is taken to a factory where heat is used to separate the metal from the ore. This process is called smelting. The ores are dumped into a blast furnace and heated to over 3000 °F (1600 °C). The metals in the ores melt and pure liquid metal sinks to the bottom. The rest of the ore is waste material called slag.

The liquid metal is poured into molds until it hardens. The bars of hardened metal are called ingots.

The ingots are ready to be rolled, pressed, or molded into the shapes of the things we use.

Practical Plastics

Look at your toys. What are they made of? Many toys are made of plastic. Plastic is easily shaped, and it lasts a long time. Hard plastic helmets protect us when we ride bikes or play sports. Rubberlike plastic is used to make balls. Soft plastics are used to make dolls. And plastic can be recycled to make long-lasting benches and picnic tables.

Plastic is not dug from the ground like metal ore. It is made from chemicals in crude oil. The chemicals in plastic can be heated so that they soften or melt. Then they are shaped into different items.

Sometimes, the chemicals are poured as liquid into molds. Once they cool, the plastic becomes solid.

A sturdy plastic cup won't break as easily as a glass one, and it's lighter.

Balls can be made by blowing air into hot, soft plastic, just like you blow up a balloon.

Many shapes can be created from plastic, such as all the parts on this toy.

Vinyl is used to make hollow parts, such as this doll's head.

A softer, movable plastic called **vinyl** (VY nihl) is used to make some toys. The molds used to make these parts are spun around so that the vinyl clings to the inside walls. The parts harden as they bake in an oven.

Playful Plastic

Let your imagination go. Snap brick after brick together and create a castle—or a spaceship. Children have played with building bricks for many years.

As you are making your cities and ships, do you ever wonder how plastic building pieces are made? They are made of a strong, tough, long-lasting plastic.

Each building piece begins as a bunch of plastic pellets. The plastic pellets are heated to 450 °F (230 °C). When they melt, they are like bread dough. Molding machines press this "dough" into different shapes and pieces.

The parts fall into bins at the end of each machine. Robots collect the full bins. They are then labeled and placed in a warehouse.

Different departments put different building kits

KNOW It All!

For some model designers, work is play! Many get to play with plastic building bricks all day. Their job is to make designs for displays at toy fairs and exhibits around the country. Sometimes these designs are over 6 feet (2 meters) high! Children love to play with toy bricks, too.

together. First, they order the pieces they need from the factory. Then, workers in each department seal the pieces in small plastic bags. The bags are sorted into boxes for the building kits. Other machines make the labels and boxes for each set.

Under Cover

When you ride your bike, you wear a helmet to protect your head. If you play baseball or other sports, you probably wear helmets or shin guards made of plastic. But did you ever think you would wear plastic clothes?

When plastics were invented, scientists learned how to make some of them into wearable fabric. For example, nylon is an **artificial** (AHR tuh FISH uhl) fabric made from plastic.

Nylon is lightweight and waterproof. That's why it is a popular fabric for outdoor clothing. When it's cold outside and the wind is blowing hard, do you put on a down jacket? If you do, chances are you're wearing plastic.

The lining of your jacket probably contains **polyester** (PAHL ee EHS tuhr). Polyester is another artificial material. It is often used in coat linings because it is durable and warm.

Many other things we wear are made from artificial fabrics. Look at your boots. Do the soles look like rubber? Today most "rubber" is made from nylon mixed with other artificial materials. Like rubber that comes from the rubber tree, it is good at keeping water out.

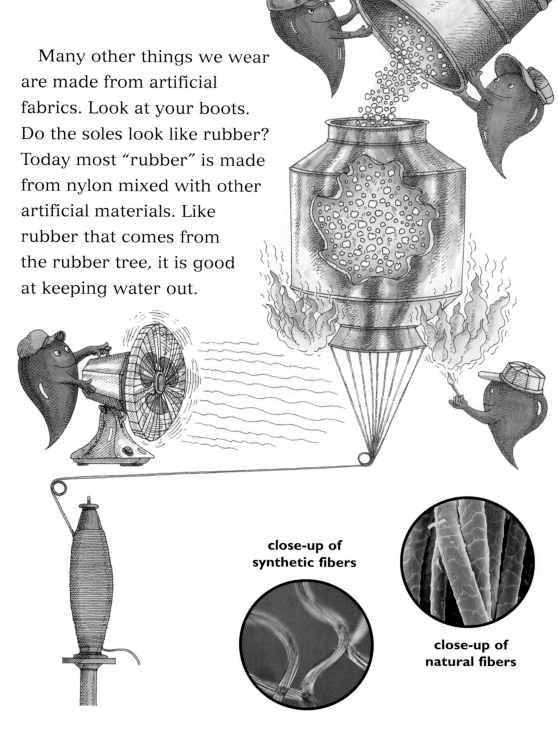

close-up of
synthetic fibers

close-up of
natural fibers

Cloth is made from long strands called fibers. Natural fibers come from such things as sheep's wool or cotton plants. Synthetic fibers are made by people.

People Who Make Things

Every day, workers in factories make the clothes we wear, the toys we play with, and the food we eat. The workers are the people on the assembly line and the people who pack and ship the products. But there are other workers involved in making products and food, too.

Does your cereal stay crispy in milk? People called food chemists (KEHM ihstz) develop and improve foods. They test new coatings or glazes to keep cereal crispy in milk. They add vitamins and minerals to make it healthier. And they

This man inspects cereal during the manufacturing process.

test different ways of cooking and packing to improve the taste or quality.

Agricultural engineers help design the machines used to make a new breakfast cereal. They might work with the food chemists to decide how the cereal will be made.

Quality technicians (tehk NIHSH uhnz) test the food for freshness. They also make sure the taste and texture of the food stay the same during production.

Plant technicians work with the people who buy the ingredients. Quality ingredients are important to make quality food. Plant technicians also work on improving how food is shipped to stores.

This man checks the final product as it rolls down a conveyer belt.

Where Would We Be Without...?

TRY THIS! 1

All these people are in big trouble! They need an invention to help them out. For example, the guy holding up his pants needs a belt. Can you name the invention that would rescue each person?

vacuum cleaner

fly swatter

elevator

safety matches

airplane

can opener

belt

fishing pole

lock and key

tissue

umbrella

aspirin

telephone

See page 181-182 for answers.

Creating and Designing

Ask your parents how they like wrinkle-free clothing. It goes from the dryer to a hanger with no ironing needed. Ask them how they like the cordless drill. They can charge the batteries and use it anywhere. Do you have a computer at school? Does it make it easier and faster for you to do your schoolwork?

All of these things were designed and created by people. They work on projects that range from building dams to designing electronics. They put science to work for us. Their ideas help us get our work done.

You can still see the wooden frame on this house that is being built.

Modern Homes

What is your home like? Are the walls made of brick, or wood, or concrete? Are the windows large or small? Does it have a shingle roof or a tile roof?

Today, most houses are made of wood, brick, and glass. The kind of materials used depends on the size of the house, its design, and the climate.

Many houses use a lot of wood. Wood is used to make the frame of the house and the frames between the walls. Sheets of wood are used for the floors and roof.

The roof is covered with tar paper and then shingled. In warm climates, ceramic tiles are used to keep the house cool. In snowy climates, the roof slopes to let the heavy snow slide off.

On the outside, many homes use aluminum or vinyl siding because it doesn't need to be painted. They can withstand cold, hot, and windy weather. Bricks also make very sturdy walls and are usually easy to get. Bricks come in many colors, too.

Large glass windows let in lots of sunshine.

Gutters are made of aluminum or plastic. They keep the water running off the roof from leaking into the house.

The house is almost finished. It has siding and a shingled roof.

The house is now complete with shutters and landscaping.

"Hidden" Between the Walls

What would you see if you could travel through the walls, under the floor, and above the ceiling in a building? Electric wires, cable TV wires, water pipes, heating ducts, gas pipes, and insulation are "hidden" between the walls. Sounds crowded, doesn't it? This drawing shows some of the different parts.

insulation

drywall

bricks

wood sheathing

heating duct

concrete foundation

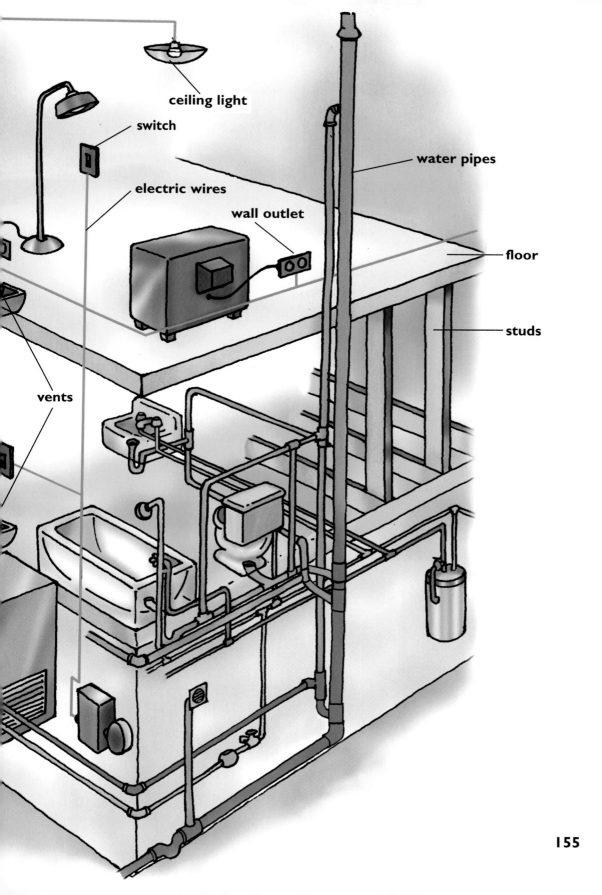

ceiling light

switch

electric wires

wall outlet

water pipes

floor

studs

vents

155

A New House

It takes a lot of work by a lot of different people to build a house. And it takes a lot of little touches to make a house feel like a home. Match each job description with the worker it describes in the picture.

TRY THIS! 1

j

1. The **architect** (AHR kuh tehkt) begins the house by drawing plans. For example, each room needs to have a door, and ceilings and doorways need to be high enough for people to walk through easily.

2. **Bulldozer operators** clear the land. They push down trees and level the ground.

3. **Carpenters** make the framework for the walls. Later, they put cabinets, doors, and woodwork in place.

4. **Concrete** (KAHN kreet) workers pour the **foundations** (fown DAY shuhnz), basement walls, sidewalks, curbs, and patios.

5. **Bricklayers** make strong walls. The bricks are held together with a kind of cement.

6. **Electricians** put wiring, electric meters, lights, and outlets in the wall frames.

7. **Plumbers** place water pipes and connect drains before the other workers cover the inside frames with wallboard or dry wall.

8. Painters help finish the inside and outside of the house.

9. Roofers install roofing tiles to keep the house dry all year.

10. Landscapers choose plants and flowers that will grow well around the house.

See page 182 for answers.

Tunnel Vision

You are building a road but a mountain is in the way. Could the road be built over the mountain? That would be rough traveling. What about going around? That would take longer—to build it and to drive on it. What about digging a tunnel? A tunnel is the shortest route, and there are many ways to build one.

Tunnels built through hard rock are usually blasted. Workers use **explosives** (ehk SPLOH sihvz) to blast each section of rock. Then they build supports in the newly opened part of the tunnel to keep rock from falling in.

Huge boring machines tunnel through clay or soft rock. As steel tubes dig through the ground, the

Explosives such as dynamite can be used to blast a tunnel through solid rock.

Holes are made in the rock.

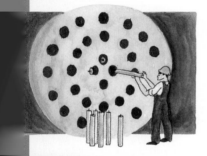

Dynamite is placed in the holes.

First, second, and third explosions make a bigger and bigger hole.

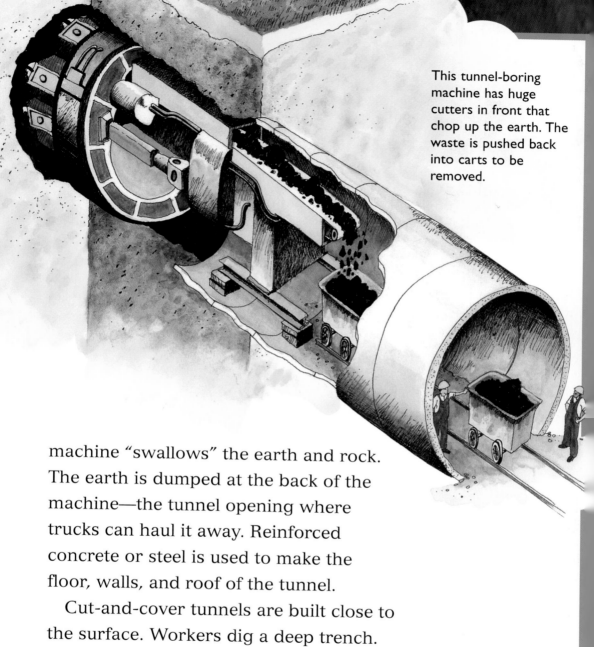

This tunnel-boring machine has huge cutters in front that chop up the earth. The waste is pushed back into carts to be removed.

machine "swallows" the earth and rock. The earth is dumped at the back of the machine—the tunnel opening where trucks can haul it away. Reinforced concrete or steel is used to make the floor, walls, and roof of the tunnel.

Cut-and-cover tunnels are built close to the surface. Workers dig a deep trench. Then they build a floor, walls, and roof of reinforced concrete. When the concrete has hardened, the area around the concrete is filled to street level.

The mountain is no longer in the way. You simply drive right through it.

Bridging the Gap

People have been using bridges to cross water for thousands of years. The earliest bridges were tree trunks. A tree growing near the shore was chopped down so that it fell across the river. Then people walked across on it. In the jungles of South America, for a long time people have made bridges out of the vines that grow there.

The ancient Romans built arched bridges out of stone. Many of them are

A long time ago, people made bridges from wood. They covered the bridges with walls and roofs. This kept snow and water from rotting the wood. Today, bridges are made mostly of steel, concrete, and other materials that don't rot.

KNOW It All!

still used today! Some bridges are still made in the same way.

Bridge-builders build strong columns, called piers, on each side of the arch. Then a strong frame is made out of wood between the piers. The arch stones are laid on top of the frame. Each stone is wedge-shaped—it is wider at the top than at the bottom. The last stone, which fits in the middle of the arch, is called the keystone. When the keystone is pushed into place, the wooden frame is taken away.

The arch will then stay in place by itself. Each stone is pressing against the next, so they hold one another up.

The Ancient Romans built many arch bridges out of stone. Bridges are still made in the same way today.

archstones

keystone

pier

wooden frame

Better Bridges

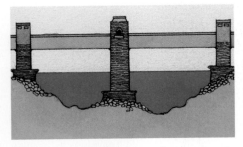

Beam bridge: This can be made of wood, steel, or concrete.

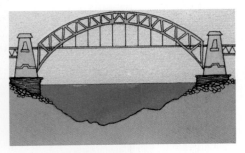

Arch bridge: A beam bridge can break easily in the middle. But a curving arch helps to carry the load on the bridge.

Thanks to bridges, rivers and lakes will not interrupt a journey. People build bridges to make it easier to cross rough land or water. There are thousands of bridges in the world, but only five basic kinds: beam, arch, suspension (suh SPEHN shuhn), cantilever (KAN tuh LEEV ur), and cable-stayed bridges.

Do you think bridges could be made out of glass? Inventors are working on this idea now. Concrete used in bridges is worn down by salt,

Suspension bridge: The roadway is suspended, or hung, from long steel cables. This type of bridge can be much longer than other types.

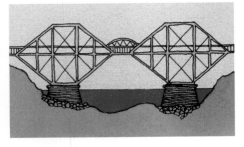

Cantilever bridge: One or more independent beams joined by a center span make a cantilever bridge.

The Sunshine Skyway Bridge in St. Petersburg, Florida, is a contemporary example of a cable-stayed bridge.

ice, and wind. The steel used to make the concrete stronger often rusts. But a special glass called fiberglass is very strong. When glass fibers are held together by a type of "glue" called resin (REH sihn), they become stronger than steel or concrete. Fiberglass is also lightweight and can be easily shaped.

Cable-stayed bridge: This is one of the newest kinds of bridge designs. It takes less concrete or steel than a beam bridge. And it fits across narrow rivers better than a suspension bridge.

Name That Bridge

Can you name the type of each bridge in this scene? Is it a beam bridge, a cable-stayed bridge, an arch bridge, a suspension bridge, or a cantilever bridge? How is each type of bridge different from the others?

See page 182 for answers.

Standing Tall

Tall trees in the forest sway in the wind. So do tall skyscrapers in the city but you just don't notice it as much. So how do these very tall buildings stay up?

The walls of a skyscraper are made of stone, concrete, glass, or metal. Under the walls is a frame of concrete or steel. This frame is strong enough to hold up the walls and floors. But it can also bend very slightly in the wind—like trees do. A tall tree has deep roots that hold up the trunk and branches. Tall buildings have deep **foundations** (fown DAY shuhnz). The foundation holds

The superstructure, the part above the ground, gives the building its shape and also supports it.

the steel girders in the ground.

The builders dig down until they find solid rock to build the foundation on. If there is no rock and the ground is soft, the basement is built on piles. Piles are deep holes bored into the ground. The holes are filled with steel and concrete. This gives the building a sturdy base to rest upon.

The part below the ground, called the substructure, supports the building's weight.

A technician stands with an android robot named Cog. Its body resembles a human being's. It can be used to study how humans interact with other people.

Engineers at Work

Our world is full of machines that help us use things, go places, and communicate. Engineers help make all this possible. Here are just a few types of engineers and what they do.

This engineer tests materials in a film lab.

Materials engineers figure out how to make the products we use better. They develop new materials for making anything from hand tools to huge trains. They also find new ways to use the materials we already have.

Mechanical engineers design new machines. Some mechanical engineers invent better ways of heating and cooling homes and buildings.

In many ways, engineers are helping to design the future.

Architectural engineers develop better ways of building homes and other buildings. They also find ways to make buildings taller.

Chemical engineers design ways to end pollution. They create drugs to fight cancer and other illnesses, too.

Civil engineering is the oldest kind of engineering. Civil engineers design bridges, subways, roads, dams, and canals.

Electrical engineers design equipment that produces electric power and sends it to our homes. They also design computer circuits and robots.

This architect uses a computer to help design buildings.

Making Way for Roads

To build new roads, workers move huge amounts of earth and rock. They flatten high ground and fill in low places.

A machine called a scraper box is used to move earth from one place to another. It is a huge open box with a slot at the bottom. The box is slung between two diesel engines. Its huge rubber tires are over 9 feet (3 meters) high.

The engine roars. The scraper lumbers over the ground. A blade at the front bites into the ground at an angle. In

This back hoe has a shovel that can move large amounts of dirt in one scoop.

seconds, over 30 tons (27 metric tons) of dirt are scraped into the box.

Powerful shovels also dig up the earth. Each scoop is as big as a bus.

This machine lays asphalt—a mixture of sand, small rocks, and tar—to pave a road.

The scraper box and shovels dump their loads, and bulldozers push the piles to fill in low spots. More rocks are rammed into the ground to make a solid base for the road.

Grading machines carefully level off the top layer of small stones. Another machine lays asphalt (AS fawlt)—a mixture of sand, small rocks, and tar. Finally, road rollers press the surface absolutely flat.

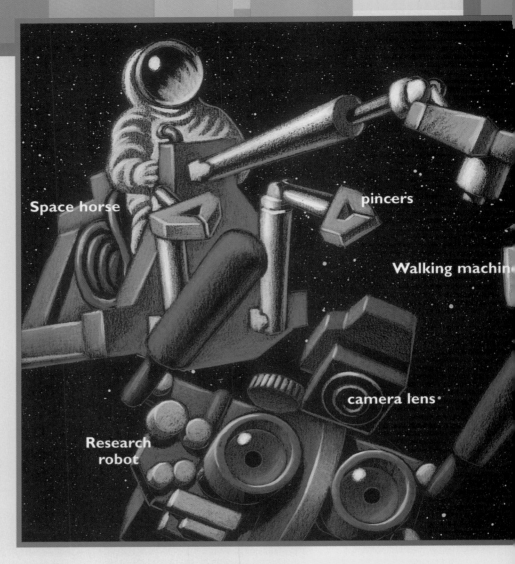

Space horse

pincers

Walking machin[e]

camera lens

Research robot

TRY THIS!
1

Roles for Robots

Robots can do many of the things people can do.
They can also walk, see, and hear in places where
people can't go. Robots are used in the deep sea,
inside volcanoes, and in space.

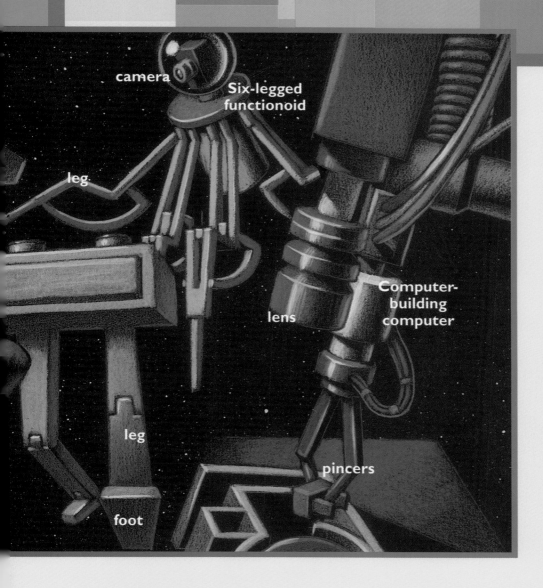

Here are some space robots. They are imaginary, but they have many of the same features that real robots have. Look at each type of robot. Does it walk, hear, see, grip, or hold?

See page 182 for answers.

How Do Robots Learn New Jobs?

With a click and a whirr, a robot keeps busy in the factory. It joins steel panels together. All day long it works on brand-new cars.

Some robots push a metal pin called a rivet through metal sheets to join the pieces together. Others are welders. They heat the edges of the metal very quickly so that they melt and join together.

There are no humans working these robots. These robots work by themselves.

How are robots able to join the parts correctly every time? First, a human teaches the robot to do the job. As the human moves the different parts of the machine in and out, up and down, reaching out and twisting around, every movement is recorded by the robot's microprocessor. Now the robot has all these movements in its memory. It knows exactly what to do every time a car is put in front of it. As long as the cars are put in exactly the same place each time, the robot will click into action and do exactly the right movements for riveting, welding, or even spray-painting.

Some robots can move around, traveling on wheels. This robot cleans the house— including washing windows!

A Helping Hand

As scientists learn more through technology, they are able to improve some of the machines we already use. Car companies hire safety engineers to make cars safer.

Doctors use technology to help people live longer and better lives. With technology, scientists have found ways to

KNOW It All!

Today some artificial limbs—arms and legs—can move and bend like real limbs. When our muscles contract, they send out electric currents. A disk inside the artificial arm or leg picks up this current. This current controls an electric motor in the artificial limb, making it bend or move.

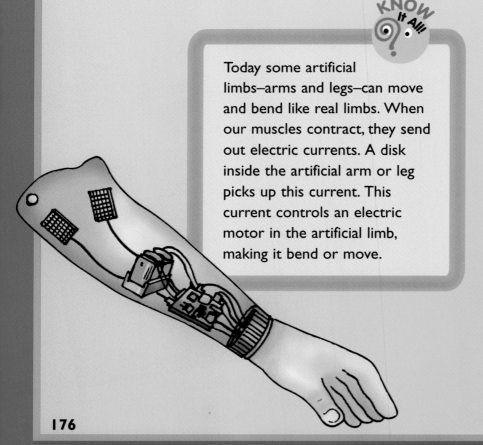

make machines that do the work of body parts, like artificial limbs. Technology may even find a way to replace sight with artificial eyes.

Technology also improves the quality of life for the disabled. For example, hearing-impaired people can read phone messages and type responses. New computer programs convert speech into commands so those with physical disabilities can now use computers.

An artificial leg makes it possible for this girl to play tennis.

Environmental workers wear protective clothing when they handle toxic, or poisonous, materials.

People expect technology to keep improving life. But some technology can be harmful. Scientists and engineers did not realize this for a long time. For example, machines are run on fuel.

The word engineer comes from the Latin word dingeniare, which means "to design" or "to create." Engineers design all kinds of things, from roads and bridges to computers and spacecraft.

Burning fuel **pollutes** (puh LOOTS) the air.

A new kind of engineering helps protect the earth from technology—and it uses technology to do it! It's called environmental engineering. Engineers in this area of research use radar to track pollution. They work on finding fuels that run machines with less pollution. They also find ways to clean up and fix the pollution technology has already made.

Airbags in the front of a car protect adult passengers in the front seat in case of an accident. If a crash occurs at about 12 miles (19 kilometers) per hour or faster, the airbag fills with a gas called nitrogen (NY truh juhn). The blown-up airbag cushions the passengers like a big pillow, keeping them from hitting the dashboard and windshield.

ANSWERS

From pages 10-11—Which Inventions Don't Belong?

The items that don't belong in the picture are the frozen food, television set, electric light bulb, digital camera, electric fan, and portable radio.

From pages 36-37—Zeroing in

Answer to binary coded message is: "on and off"

From pages 42-43—What Machines Do They Need?

a. paint roller
b. wagon
c. lawn mower
d. sewing machine
e. grill
f. tandem bike
g. watch
h. computer
i. fan
j. sprinkler

From pages 46-47—Machines that Move Things

1. potter's wheel
2. grocery cart
3. crane
4. escalator
5. stroller
6. mixer
7. tractor-semitrailer
8. elevator
9. conveyor belt
10. fork lift

From pages 58-59—Truckin'

a. A tow truck tows a car.

b. A moving van carries furniture.

c. A garbage truck carries garbage.

d. A bottler carries bottled liquids

e. A mail truck carries mail.

f. A dump truck carries dirt.

g. A ready-mix concrete truck carries wet concrete.

h. A motor home carries a family.

From pages 80-81—What Makes It Fly?

rocket: 2, 7, 9

helicopter: 1, 3, 8

jet plane: 5, 6, 10

propeller plane: 3, 4, 5, 6

From pages 108-109—Does It Send or Receive?

1. clock radio: receive
2. pay phone: both
3. microphone: send
4. garage door opener: send
5. walkie-talkie: both
6. home satellite dish: receive
7. personal stereo: receive
8. cellular phone: both
9. radio-controlled car: receive
10. pager: both
11. TV remote control: send

From pages 148-149—Where Would We Be Without...?

a. tissue

b. vacuum cleaner

c. umbrella

d. fly swatter

e. can opener

f. safety matches

g. elevator

h. airplane

i. aspirin

j. telephone

k. lock and key

l. belt

m. fishing pole

From pages 156-157—A New House

1. Architect: f
2. Bulldozer operator: i
3. Carpenter:g
4. Concrete worker: h
5. Bricklayer: b
6. Electrician: d
7. Plumber: e
8. Painter: c
9. Roofer: a
10. Landscaper: j

From page 164-165—Name That Bridge

1. cable-stayed
2. beam
3. arch
4. arch
5. beam
6. cable-stayed
7. suspension
8. cantilever
9. suspension
10. cantilever

From pages 172-173—Roles for Robots

Space horse: grips, holds

Research robot: sees

Walking machine: walks

Six-legged functionoid: sees, walks

Computer-building computer: holds, grips, sees

Glossary

Here are some of the words you read in this book. Many of them may be new to you. Some are hard to pronounce. But since you will see them again, they are good words to know. Next to each word, you will see how to say it correctly: **amplifier** (AM pluh FY uhr). The part shown in small capital letters is said a little more loudly than the rest of the word. The part in large capital letters is said the loudest. Under each word are one or two sentences that tell what the word means.

A

amplifier (AM pluh FY uhr)
An amplifier is a tool or machine that increases the loudness of a sound.

artificial (AHR tuh FIHSH uhl)
If something is artificial, it has been made by people. It is not part of nature.

assembly line (uh SEHM blee lyn)
An assembly line consists of a row of workers and machines, or robots, that put something together, each adding a different part.

B

buoyancy (BOY uhn see)
Buoyancy is the force that makes something float.

C

calculator (KAL kyuh LAY tuhr)
A calculator is a machine able to do mathematical problems.

carbon (KAHR buhn)
Carbon is a chemical element. Sometimes carbon is a powdery or crumbly black material. Coal is mostly carbon.

chemist (KEHM ihst)
A chemist is a person trained in the study of elements and how they change when they are mixed together.

circuit (SUR kiht)
A circuit is a path along which an electric current flows.

combustion (kuhm BUHS chuhn)
Combustion is the process of catching fire and burning.

concrete (KAHN kreet)
Concrete is a building material made by mixing cement, sand, gravel, and water.

condense (kuhn DEHNS)
To condense something is to change it from a gas to a liquid. Steam condenses to water when it cools.

conducting (kuhn DUHK tihng)
Conducting means carrying or transferring energy.

D

diaphragm (DY uh fram)
A diaphragm is a thin disk or cone that vibrates when sound hits it.

digital code (DIHJ uh tuhl kohd)
Digital code is a series of numbers that stands for instructions.

E

engineer (EHN juh NIHR)
An engineer is a person trained to design and make things, such as buildings, bridges, machines, electrical equipment, and chemicals.

environmental (ehn VY ruhn MEHN tuhl)
Environmental means having to do with the relationships among living things.

escalator (EHS kuh LAY tuhr)
An escalator is a moving stairway.

evaporate (ih VAP uh rayt)
To evaporate is to change from a liquid to a gas. Water evaporates when it boils away.

explosives (ehk SPLOH sihvz)
Explosives are materials that blow up. Explosives are used to break up rock in mines and tunnels.

F

foundation (fown DAY shuhn)
A foundation is something used as a base or support to hold something up.

frequency (FREE kwuhn see)
Frequency is the number of times an electric current or other wave vibrates every second.

G

gas (gas)
A gas is one of three forms of matter. Gases spread out in all directions to fill up space.

gravity (GRAV uh tee)
Gravity is the force that pulls things toward the earth.

I

infrared (IHN fruh REHD)
Infrared rays are rays with wavelengths longer than those of red light. The human eye is unable to see infrared rays.

integrated circuit (IHN tuh GRAY tihd SUR kiht)
An integrated circuit is a tiny chip filled with electrical switches that can hold all the signals needed to run electronic devices. It is another name for a microchip.

inventor (ihn VEHN tuhr)
An inventor is a person who creates something new.

L

laser beam (LAY zuhr beem)
A laser beam is a special kind of light. The beam is very narrow and powerful.

M

magnetic (mag NEHT ihk)
If something is magnetic, it has the ability to attract bits of iron and steel.

magnetize (MAG nuh tyz)
To magnetize something is to make it magnetic.

microchip (MY kroh CHIHP)
A microchip is a tiny chip filled with electrical switches that can hold all the signals needed to run electronic devices. It is another name for an integrated circuit.

microprocessor (MY kroh PRAHS uhs uhr)
A microprocessor is a tiny computer "brain" that fits on a microchip. A microprocessor can do all the things needed to run an electronic gadget.

microwave (MY kroh wayv)
Microwave is a form of energy. A microwave is a very short, superhigh-frequency radio wave.

modem (MOH duhm)
A modem is a device used to convert information from words or images to digital code and back again.

O

oxidizer (AHK suh DY zuhr)
An oxidizer is something that helps cause a reaction, such as the burning of fuel or the rusting of metal.

P

pollute (puh LOOT)
To pollute is to make the air, earth, or water impure or dirty.

polyester (PAHL ee EHS tuhr)
Polyester is an artificial fiber used to make wrinkle-free clothing.

pressure (PREHSH uhr)
Pressure is a force caused by pushing on or against something.

R

radar (RAY dahr)
A radar machine uses reflected radio waves to tell the distance, direction, and speed of objects.

radio wave (RAY dee oh wayv)
A radio wave is an electric signal that vibrates millions of times per second as it travels.

resist (rih ZIHST)
To resist is to slow down or to work against a type of force. Some materials resist electric currents.

S

sensor (SEHN suhr)
A sensor is any device that sends out signals to detect changes in temperature, movement, or something else.

silicon (SIHL uh kuhn)
Silicon is a chemical element. It is used to make computer chips and other things.

T

technician (tehk NIHSH uhn)
A technician is a person with special skills in a particular area, such as computers.

technology (tehk NAHL uh jee)
Technology includes all the machines and ways of doing things people have invented to make work and life easier.

thermometer (thuhr MAHM uh tuhr)
A thermometer is a machine or device used for measuring temperature.

transportation (trans puhr TAY shuhn)
Transportation is the action of carrying people or goods from one place to another.

turbine (TUHR byn)
A turbine is a motor with blades that spin. The spinning blades can power an airplane or other machine.

V

vibrate (VY brayt)
To vibrate is to move back and forth quickly. Sounds are made by things that vibrate.

vinyl (VY nuhl)
Vinyl is a strong but soft plastic. It is used to make clothing, floor coverings, and toys.

Index

This index is an alphabetical list of important topics covered in this book. It will help you find information given in both words and pictures. To help you understand what an entry means, there is sometimes a helping word in parentheses, for example, **belt** (clothing). If there is information in both words and pictures, you will see the words *with pictures* in parentheses after the page number. If there is only a picture, you will see the word *picture* in parentheses after the page number.

agitator, in washing machine, 20 *(with picture)*
agricultural engineer, 147
airbag, 179
aircraft carrier, 69 *(picture)*
airplane, 12, 148 *(picture)*
  flight by, 74-75, 81 *(with pictures)*
  on ship, 69 *(with picture)*
  propeller, 74, 81 *(with picture)*
  tracking location of, 94-95 *(with picture)*
  see also **jet plane**
air traffic controller, 94-95 *(with picture)*
alarm, security, 96-97 *(with picture)*
alphabet, and digital code, 36-37
American Orient Express (train), 61 *(picture)*
amplifier, 28-29, 89
answering machine, 35 *(picture)*
Arabs, and cheese, 123
arch bridge, 160-162 *(with pictures)*
architect, 156 *(with picture)*
architectural engineer, 169 *(with picture)*
arm, artificial, 176 *(picture)*
artificial limb, 177 *(with pictures)*
artist, and car design, 82
asphalt, 171
aspirin, 149 *(picture)*
assembly line, 83 *(with pictures),* 146 *(with pictures)*
automobile, see **car**

bakery, 118-119
ball (toy), 141 *(picture)*
bandage, adhesive, 12 *(with picture)*
Banff National Park (Canada), 60 *(picture)*
beam bridge, 162 *(with picture)*
beater brush, 23
beeper, see **pager**
Bell, Alexander Graham (inventor), 100

belt (clothing), 149 *(picture)*
bicycle, 42 *(picture),* 50-51 *(with pictures)*
binary code, see **digital code**
blast furnace, 138 *(picture)*
blue (color), 90
brakes
  car, 54 *(with picture)*
  motorcycle, 53
bread, 118-119 *(with pictures)*
brick (material), 152-154 *(with picture)*
  see also **building bricks**
bricklayer, 156 *(with picture)*
bridge (structure), 160-165 *(with pictures)*
building bricks, 142-143 *(with pictures)*
bulldozer operator, 156 *(with picture)*
buoyancy, 64

cable-stayed bridge, 162 *(with pictures)*
cable television, 89 *(with picture)*
CAD, see **computer-aided design**
calculator (machine), 35 *(with picture)*
caller ID, 101 *(with picture)*
camera
  digital, 11 *(picture)*
  television, 88-89
can opener, 148 *(picture)*
cantilever bridge, 162 *(with picture)*
car
  designing, 82-83 *(with pictures)*
  parts of, 54-55 *(with pictures)*
  robot in manufacturing, 174-175 *(with picture)*
carbon, in telephone, 100 *(with picture)*
carbon dioxide, in bread, 119
careers
  construction, 156-157 *(with picture)*

engineering, see **engineer**
  manufacturing, 146-147 *(with pictures)*
carpenter, 156 *(with picture)*
cassette tape, 28-29 *(with picture)*
CD (recording), see **compact disc**
CD-ROM, 38, 40-41 *(with picture)*
cell (area), 102-103
cellular telephone, 84 *(picture),* 102-103 *(with picture),* 109 *(picture)*
Celsius (temperature), 15
cement mixer, 44 *(picture)*
cereal, 146-147 *(with pictures)*
chair, 11 *(picture)*
cheese, 122-123 *(with picture)*
chemical engineer, 169 *(with picture)*
chemist, 146-147
China (country), **pottery in,** 132
circuit (electronics), 35
civil engineer, 169 *(with picture)*
clay, 110, 132-133 *(with pictures)*
clock, 35 *(picture)*
clock radio, 108 *(picture)*
cloth, see **fabric**
clothes
  for motorcyclists, 53 *(picture)*
  in washing machine, 20-21 *(with pictures)*
  materials for, 134-135 *(with pictures),* 144-145 *(with pictures)*
code, for security system, 96
  see also **digital code**
coil, heating, 18 *(with pictures),* 25 *(with picture)*
cold, from refrigerator, 16-17 *(with pictures)*
color, and television, 88-89
combustion chamber (rocket), 79
compact disc, 30-31 *(with pictures)*
  see also **CD-ROM**
computer, 8 *(picture),* 38-39 *(with pictures),* 42 *(picture)*
  car design with, 82-83 *(with pictures)*
  for disabled, 177

Internet and, 106-107 *(with picture)*
microchip in, 34 *(picture)*, 35 *(picture)*
phone messages with, 98
computer-aided design, 82-83 *(with pictures)*
Concorde (airplane), 75 *(picture)*
concrete, 154 *(with picture)*, 156 *(with picture)*, 159, 162-163
concrete worker, 156 *(with picture)*
condensation, 16-17
conduction, 24
conveyor belt, 47 *(picture)*, 117 *(with picture)*, 118 *(with pictures)*
cotton, 134 *(with picture)*
crane (machine), 47 *(picture)*
crankshaft (car), 57 *(with picture)*
cruise liner (ship), 68
cup, 136, 140 *(picture)*
curd, 123
cylinder (car), 57 *(with picture)*
Cyprus (island), 133 *(picture)*

Daimler, Gottlieb (inventor), 53
da Vinci, Leonardo, *see* **Leonardo da Vinci**
Delta rocket, 78 *(picture)*
design, 150 *(with picture)*
 see also **computer-aided design; engineer**
diaphragm (telephone), 100-101 *(with picture)*
Dickson, Earle (inventor), 12
digital camera, 11 *(picture)*
digital code, 30-31, 36-39 *(with picture)*, 106
digital thermometer, 14-15 *(with picture)*
digital video disc, 40 *(with picture)*
disabled, 177 *(with picture)*
doll, 141 *(picture)*
drywall (material), 154 *(picture)*
DVD (recording), 40 *(with picture)*

Edison, Thomas A. (inventor), 12 *(with picture)*
electrical engineer, 169 *(with picture)*
electrical signal, 31, 100-101
electric current
 in hair dryer, 24-25
 in microprocessor, 35
 in telephone wire, 100-101
electrician, 156 *(with picture)*
electromagnet, 86, 101
electron gun, 89

electronic keyboard, 35 *(picture)*
electronic mail, *see* **e-mail**
elevator, 47 *(picture)*, 148 *(picture)*
e-mail, 98, 107
engine
 car, 55 *(picture)*, 56-57 *(with pictures)*
 jet, 74-75
 motorcycle, 53
 rocket, 78-79 *(with picture)*
 train, 62-63
 see also **motor**
engineer, 83, 168-169 *(with pictures)*, 179
 agricultural, 147
 environmental, 179
environmental engineer, 179
environmental worker, 178 *(picture)*
escalator, 46 *(picture)*, 48-49 *(with picture)*
evaporation, 16-17
explosive, 158 *(with picture)*

fabric, 134-135 *(with pictures)*, 144-145 *(with pictures)*
factory
 assembly line in, 83 *(with pictures)*, 146 *(with pictures)*
 workers in, 146-147 *(with pictures)*
Fahrenheit (temperature), 15
fan (machine), 11 *(picture)*, 42 *(picture)*
 hairdryer, 25 *(with picture)*
 vacuum cleaner, 23 *(with picture)*
fax machine, 98 *(with picture)*
fiber
 natural, 134-135 *(with pictures)*, 145 *(picture)*
 synthetic, 144-145 *(with pictures)*
fiberglass, 83, 163
fireworks, 79 *(with picture)*
firing (pottery), 133
fishing pole, 149 *(picture)*
fishing ship, 69
flight
 airplane, 74-75, 81 *(with pictures)*
 helicopter, 72-73 *(with pictures)*, 81 *(with picture)*
 rocket, 78-79 *(with picture)*, 81 *(with picture)*
floating, 64-65 *(with pictures)*
floor, of house, 155 *(picture)*
fly swatter, 148 *(picture)*
food
 frozen, 11 *(picture)*
 processing of, 116-125 *(with picture)*
fork lift, 46 *(picture)*

foundation, of building, 154 *(picture)*, 156, 166-167 *(with picture)*
freighter (ship), 69
freight train, 60 *(with picture)*
frequency, wave, 86, 93
fuel
 for car, 57
 for train, 63
 pollution and, 178-179

garage-door opener, 93, 109 *(picture)*
gas
 in car engine, 57
 in refrigerator, 16-17 *(with picture)*
gear
 in bicycle, 51 *(with pictures)*
 in escalator, 48-49 *(picture)*
gearshift, 55 *(with picture)*
generator, in car, 55 *(with picture)*
glass, 136-137 *(with pictures)*
 in house, 152
 see also **fiberglass**
glass blower, 137 *(picture)*
glazing, of pottery, 133
grading machine, 171 *(with picture)*
green (color), 90
grill (appliance), 43 *(picture)*
grocery cart, 47 *(picture)*
gutter, of house, 153

hairdryer, 24-25 *(with pictures)*
headphones, 87 *(picture)*
heat, from hairdryer, 24-25
heating duct, 154 *(picture)*
helicopter, 12, 44 *(picture)*, 72-73 *(with pictures)*, 81 *(with picture)*
 on ship, 69 *(with picture)*
helmet, 53 *(with pictures)*
hologram, 32 *(with pictures)*
house, 152-157 *(with pictures)*

ice cream, 124-125 *(with pictures)*
ignition, car, 56 *(with picture)*
infrared rays, 15, 31, 93
ingot, 139
injector, in car, 57 *(with picture)*
inkjet printer, 39
insulation, in house, 154 *(picture)*
integrated circuit, 35
Internet, 106-107 *(with picture)*
Internet Service Provider, 107
invention, 8-12 *(with pictures)*, 148-149 *(with pictures)*
 see also specific inventions

inventor, 12-13 *(with pictures)*
ISP (company), 107

jet plane, 74-75 *(with pictures)*, 80 *(picture)*
jute, 135 *(picture)*

key, 149 *(picture)*
keyboard, 35 *(picture)*
keystone, 161 *(with picture)*
kiln, 133

LAN (network), 106 *(picture)*
landscaper, 157 *(with picture)*
laser
  in compact disc player, 30 *(with picture)*, 41 *(with picture)*
  in hologram, 32-33 *(with pictures)*
  in phone system, 99
laser printer, 39 *(with picture)*
lawn mower, 42 *(picture)*
leg, artificial, 177 *(picture)*
Leonardo da Vinci (inventor), 12 *(with picture)*
light bulb, 10 *(picture)*, 12 *(with picture)*
linen, 134-135 *(with picture)*
liquid, in refrigerator, 16-17 *(with picture)*
local area network, 107 *(picture)*
lock, 149 *(picture)*
L1011 Tristan (airplane), 74 *(picture)*
lye, 131

machine, *see* **invention**
magnet, electric, *see* **electromagnet**
magnetic tape, 28-29 *(with picture)*
magnet raft (project), 66-67 *(with pictures)*
manufacturing, 146-147 *(with pictures)*
map, air-traffic control, 95 *(picture)*
Marconi, Guglielmo (inventor), 86 *(with picture)*
match, safety, 148 *(picture)*
materials engineer, 169 *(with picture)*
mechanical engineer, 169 *(with picture)*
metal, 138-139 *(with pictures)*
microchip, 34-35 *(with picture)*
microphone, 108 *(picture)*

microprocessor, 34-35 *(with picture)*, 39
microwave, 99
microwave oven, 35 *(picture)*
mirror, and hologram, 32 *(with picture)*
mixer, electric, 46 *(picture)*
modem, 98, 106
monorail, 62
motion alarm, 97
motor
  escalator, 49 *(with picture)*
  vacuum cleaner, 22-23 *(with picture)*
  washing machine, 21 *(with pictures)*
  see also **engine**
motorcycle, 52-53 *(with pictures)*

network, computer, 106-107 *(with picture)*
nuclear reactor, 70
nylon (material), 144

optical fiber, 99 *(with picture)*
ore, 139
oxidizer, 78, 79
oxygen, as fuel, 78

pager, 102, 109 *(picture)*
painter, 157 *(with picture)*
paint roller, 42 *(picture)*
paper, 126-129 *(with pictures)*
paper bag, 12
parachute, 12 *(with picture)*
passenger train, 60-61 *(with picture)*
patent, 13
peanut butter, 116-117 *(with pictures)*
Pettee, S. E. (inventor), 12
piano, 11 *(picture)*
pier, 161 *(with picture)*
pile (structure), 167
piston, in car, 56-57 *(with picture)*
pixel, 90-91 *(with pictures)*
pizza, 123 *(picture)*
plane, *see* **airplane**
plant technician, 147
plastics, 140-145 *(with pictures)*
plumber, 156 *(with picture)*
pollution, from technology, 178-179 *(with pictures)*
polyester, 144
potter's wheel, 47 *(picture)*, 132 *(picture)*
pottery, 132-133 *(with pictures)*

Prague (Czech Republic), 62 *(picture)*
pressure, water, 64-65
printer (machine), 39 *(with picture)*
processed food, 116-123 *(with pictures)*
program, computer, 39, 106
propeller
  airplane, 74, 81 *(with picture)*
  helicopter, 72 *(with pictures)*, 80 *(with picture)*
pumping station, 113 *(with picture)*

quality technician, 147

radar, 94-95, 97
radio, 10 *(picture)*, 86 *(with pictures)*
radio-controlled car (toy), 93, 109 *(picture)*
radio transmitter, 86, 97, 102-103
radio wave
  in radio, 86
  in remote control, 93
  in telephone system, 99, 102-103
  in television, 89
  satellite as transmitter of, 104-105 *(with picture)*
  see also **radar**
railroad, *see* **train**
raw materials, 110 *(with picture)*
recumbent bicycle, 51 *(with picture)*
recycling, of paper, 127-129 *(with pictures)*
red (color), 89-90
refrigerator, 16-17 *(with pictures)*
remote control, 84 *(picture)*, 92-93 *(with pictures)*, 109 *(picture)*
rescue helicopter, 73 *(with picture)*
resin, 163
resistance (electricity), 24
road building, 170-171 *(with pictures)*
robot, 168 *(picture)*, 172-175 *(with pictures)*
rocket, 44 *(picture)*, 78-79 *(with pictures)*, 81 *(with picture)*
rolling machine, 139 *(with pictures)*
Rome, ancient, bridges in, 160-161 *(with picture)*
roof, of house, 152-153 *(with pictures)*
roofer, 157 *(with picture)*
rubber, 145

saltpeter (fuel), 79

sand, 110
in glassmaking, 136
satellite, artificial, 104-105 (with picture)
satellite dish, 84 (picture), 89 (with picture), 109 (picture)
Saturn V (rocket), 79
scraper box (machine), 170-171 (with picture)
security system, 96-97 (with pictures)
semitrailer truck, 46 (picture)
sensor, 21
sewing machine, 8 (picture), 35 (picture), 42 (picture)
ship, 68-69 (with pictures), 139 (picture)
floating by, 64 (with picture), 65 (with picture)
siding, on house, 153 (with pictures)
signal (electronics), 84-109 (with pictures)
magnetic tape, 28-29
remote control, 92-93
security system, 96-97 (with pictures)
telephone, 98-99, 102-103
television, 89
see also radar; radio
silicon, 35
silk, 135 (with picture)
silkworm, 135 (with picture)
skyscraper, 166-167 (with picture)
smelting, 139
soap, 130-131 (with pictures)
sound, recording of, 28-31 (with pictures)
space travel, by rocket, 34
spark plug, 57 (with picture)
sprinkler, 42 (picture)
sprocket, 50-51 (with picture)
starter motor, 56 (with picture)
steam engine, 63 (with picture)
steel, 163
steering wheel, 55 (with picture)
stereo (machine), 35 (picture), 109 (picture)
stone bridge, 160-161 (with picture)
Strasburg Rail Road, 62 (picture)
stroller, 46 (picture)
submarine, 70 (with picture)
subway, 63 (picture)
Sunshine Skyway Bridge (Florida), 163 (picture)
suspension, in car, 54 (with picture)
suspension bridge, 162 (with picture)

tandem bicycle, 42 (picture)
tanker, 69 (with picture)
tape recorder, 28-29 (with pictures)
technician, 147, 168 (picture)
technology
dangers of, 178-179 (with picture)
helping people, 176-177 (with pictures)
see also invention
telephone, 8 (picture), 11 (picture), 100-101 (with pictures), 149 (picture)
microprocessor in, 34 (with picture)
pay, 108 (picture)
signal line for, 98-99 (with picture)
see also cellular telephone
telescope, 10 (picture)
television, 10 (picture), 35 (picture), 88-89 (with pictures)
remote control, 92-93 (with pictures)
temperature, measurement of, 14-15 (with pictures)
thermometer, 14-15 (with pictures)
three-dimensional image, 32-33
tissue, 149 (picture)
toaster, 9 (picture), 18-19 (with pictures)
toilet, 26-27 (with picture)
toy
plastic, 140 (with pictures), 142-143 (with picture)
radio-controlled, 93, 109 (picture)
track, train, 61 (with picture)
train, 45 (picture), 60-63 (with pictures)
transmission, car, 55 (with picture)
transmitter, see radio transmitter
transportation, machines for, 44-83 (with pictures)
see also specific machines
Triton (submarine), 70
trolley, 62 (picture)
truck, 44 (picture), 58-59 (with pictures)
tugboat, 68 (picture)
tunnel, 158-159 (with pictures)
tunnel-boring machine, 158-159 (with picture)
turbine, 76-77 (with pictures)
jet, 75
TV, see television

umbrella, 149 (picture)
unicycle, 51 (with picture)

vacuum, 23
vacuum cleaner, 22-23 (with picture), 148 (picture)
vent
house, 154 (picture)
submarine, 70 (with picture)
vibration
sound, 30-31, 86
telephone diaphragm, 100
videocassette recorder, 35 (picture)
videotape, 29 (with picture)
vinyl, 141 (with picture)

wagon, 42 (picture)
walkie-talkie, 109 (picture)
WAN (network), 106
washing machine, 20-21 (with pictures)
Washington, D.C., 63 (picture)
watch, 35 (picture)
water
factory treatment of, 112-115 (with pictures)
floating on, 64-65 (with pictures)
in toilet, 26-27 (with picture)
in washing machine, 20-21 (with pictures)
water filter, 113-115 (with pictures)
water pipe, in house, 155 (picture)
water tower, 113 (with picture)
waterworks (factory), 113 (with picture)
wide area network, 106 (picture)
window
house, 153
security system and, 97
wood, 110
bridges of, 160
in homes, 152 (with picture)
paper from, 126-127 (with picture)
wool, 135 (with picture)
worker, see careers

yeast, 119

Illustration Acknowledgments

The Publishers of *Childcraft* gratefully acknowledge the courtesy of the following illustrators, photographers, agencies, and organizations for illustrations in this volume. When all the illustrations for a sequence of pages are from a single source, the inclusive page numbers are given. Credits should be read from top to bottom, left to right, on their respective pages. All illustrations are the exclusive property of the publishers of *Childcraft* unless names are marked with an asterisk (*).

Cover	Paddle wheel—© Cathy Melloan*; Chips and computer— G. Brian Karas; Diesel train— © Walter Rawlings, Robert Harding Picture Library*
Back Cover	G. Brian Karas
1	G. Brian Karas; © Walter Rawlings, Robert Harding Picture Library*
2-3	Joe Lemonnier; Eileen Mueller Neill
4-5	© Flax Art Supply Company*
6-7	Eileen Mueller Neill; Rick Incrocci
8-9	Eileen Mueller Neill; Carol Whiting; WORLD BOOK photo by Steve Hale
10-11	Lydia Halverson
12-13	© Flax Art Supply Company*; Rick Incrocci; Reale Library, Turin, Italy, SCALA from Art Resource*; Ambrosiana Library, Milan*; Rick Incrocci
14-15	Robert Byrd; © Leonard Lessin, Peter Arnold, Inc.*
16-17	Eileen Mueller Neill; WORLD BOOK illustration; Kathy Clo; © Novastock, Photo Researchers*
18-19	WORLD BOOK photo by Steve Hale; Rick Incrocci
20-21	Frank James; Eileen Mueller Neill; Frank James; Eileen Mueller Neill
22-23	Eileen Mueller Neill
24-25	John Sandford; WORLD BOOK illustration
26-27	Eileen Mueller Neill
28-29	WORLD BOOK illustration; WORLD BOOK photo by Jeff Guerrant; Len Ebert
30-31	© Philippe Plailly/SPL from Photo Researchers*; Rick Incrocci
32-33	© Museum of Holography, Chicago, IL*; WORLD BOOK illustration; Rick Incrocci
34-35	© Nelson Morris, Science Photo Library*; © Andrew Syred/Spl from Photo Researchers*; WORLD BOOK illustration
38-39	© Will & Deni McIntyre, Photo Researchers; Rick Incrocci
40-41	C-Cube Microsystems*; Rick Incrocci
42-43	Carl Whiting
44-45	Eileen Mueller Neill; Joe Lemonnier; Frank James; © David Barnes, Tony Stone Images*
46-47	Joe Lemonnier
48-49	Robert Byrd
50-51	Jeremy Gower; © David Young-Wolff, PhotoEdit*; Eileen Mueller Neill; © Mark A. Johnson, The Stock Market*
52-53	Lydia Halverson; Lydia Halverson; Eileen Mueller Neill
54-55	Frank James
56-57	Estelle Carol
58-59	Joe Lemonnier
60-61	© David Barnes, Tony Stone Images*; © Alison Wright, Photo Researchers*
62-63	© Rafael Macia, Photo Researchers*; © Jerry Irwin, Photo Researchers*; © Cosmo Condina, Tony Stone Images*
64-65	© F. Burmann*; © Wernher Krutein, Liaison Agency*; Eileen Mueller Neill; Roland Berry
66-67	Eileen Mueller Neill
68-69	© Superstock*; © Robert Harding Picture Library*; © Superstock*
70-71	Richard Hook; Malcom Livingstone
72-73	Frank James; © Michael Sewell, Peter Arnold. Inc.*
74-75	© Superstock*; © J. Bentley, Zefa Picture Library*
76-77	Rick Incrocci;